A LORTON
PRISON PROJECT

A Lorton Prison Project

Carolyn Williams

To order additional copies of this book, contact:
Xlibris LLC
1-888-795-4274
www.Xlibris.com
Orders@Xlibris.com
141161

DEDICATION

This is for my daughter, Desiree

BIOGRAPHICAL PROFILE

This story captures the insight of a bright, intuitively smart young man who grew up in the low-income housing projects of Southeast, Washington, D.C. our nation's capital city. His name was Jimmy Black Blango, or better known as JB. He lived in the Barry Farms Housing projects at the height of a glorified drug market, in the midst of a culture of the celebrated thug life, gang violence, and mob-style crime. Aside from all that, it was a known fact that gang bangers pledged allegiance to serving time in jail. Even JB got caught up in an operation clean sweep on the streets of Washington, D.C., and was sent down to Lorton to serve his time. From there, his status on the streets of Washington, D.C., were upgraded to include street credits (i.e., the status of lieutenant) for serving a stench at what was once called the most notorious prison on the East Coast, the Lorton Correctional Complex. Now, that the prison was mandated by federal law to shut down, the criminal element on the outside decided to bring their drug enterprise on the inside. This in an effort to establish networks that reached beyond the District, and extended to all points targeted south.

Yet due to the pending closure of the Lorton Complex and the greed amongst thieves, backstabbing gangbangers, cold-blooded killers, malicious cutthroat staffers, etc., caused the whole scam to blow up. At the end of the day, a nefarious culmination of unsavory conduct caused many elements of the Lorton Complex to suffer its unfortunate demise.

ACKNOWLEDGMENTS

I thank God first and foremost for which, without him, this project would have not been possible. I thank God for my exceptionally bright, precocious, yet, charming daughter, Desiree Shanae Williams, who is a senior at East Carolina University (Hey, go, Pirates)! Inevitably, it was her insight and forethought that has proven to be the niche that guided my beacon through the storm. I want to thank all of my family (i.e., the Gray family) and friends for their kind words of support and encouragement. I want to thank Ms. Valerie Feimster Montgomery, a graphic arts instructor at Chicago Art Institute, Ms. Tonya Nicole Gray, a recent recipient of her masters of arts degree in humanities and fine arts (an exceptional teacher at Carver Heights Elementary School, Goldsboro, N.C.), and Mrs. Ayesha Young, wife of Minister Christopher Young. She is a graduate of North Carolina A&T University, with a bachelor of science in social work / child protective services, all of whom made valuable contributions toward this project. I thank a loving family that has always shown me their love and support. I want to thank my mother, Ms. Susie Mae Gray, and my aunt, Ms. Pearlie Mae Gray, both of whom helped raise me and showered me with their love. I thank my sisters, Jackie Celestine Gray, Ms. Brenda K. Avery, and Ms. Debra A. Gray, as well as nieces, nephews, and friends. To my favorite nephews, Jashaun Newkirk and Christopher Young, keep your anchors grounded in the love, grace, and mercy of Almighty God. I also want to thank my husband, Mr. Charles M. Williams Jr., who stands by my side with lots of love and support despite my storms.

A LORTON
PRISON PROJECT:

FEATURING

JIMMY BLACK BLANGO

The present circumstance which presses so hard against you is the best-shaped tool in the father's hand to chisel you for eternity. Do not push away the instrument lest you lose its work. The school of suffering graduates rare scholars . . . the Lord designs that we shall come forth as gold, graduating with distinction.—Author unknown

This is for my daughter, Desiree Shanae Williams. I vividly remember her being given an assignment by her first grade teacher, Mrs. Urkums, at Fort Washington Forest Elementary School, Forestville. Maryland. Her class was told to write down the name of their hero. From there, Desiree immediately raised her hand and said, "I know the answer. That's easy. Let me tell you about my hero. She is honest, encouraging, reliable, and obscure. She is my mom. My mom is my hero." And with that being said, I say thank you, Desiree, because you are my hero too.

The prison is the quintessential foundation of humanity, yet, separated from the mainstream society. So, what does a child do when they are suddenly separated from their parents? They cry! Their cries are only the beginning. We must then find what level of nurturing will be required to make that child whole again! If not, we as a society will remain at war with the enemy from within.—Carolyn Williams

---

It is appointed unto men once to die, but after this the judgment (Heb. 9:27). What will be your judgment? Is it already foretold or predestined by a given set of circumstances, yet still remaining both fluid and ordained or perhaps? Is it governed by your own autonomy? Ultimately, we as human beings believe that we determine the outcome of our destiny. This concept has never been more evident or profound until it was recently determined that forces unknown to mankind have powers that override the choices we make. And from there, a separate agenda is imparted. Their goals have remained unknown since the beginning of time. In fact, postpartumly, inherent goals for this particular pathway were keenly surmised from readings such as "The Master Game" by Graham Hancock and Robert Bauval and "How to be Blessed and Highly Favored," by Michelle Mckinney Hammond.

In hindsight, on the day in question, it started out as a routine ordinary day with all the bells and whistles of the morning rise and shine. It's 6:30 a.m. and I love the morning time. To me, I'm getting a head start on activities that I must complete for each day. For me, it's like cheating restrictions governed by the confines of an allotted time that's ordained by universal law. In fact, I operated within the confines of an institution for the better part of all my young adult life, the long lost voice of a walk with destiny fills the gaps of my wayward career path that is mounted each day of my life. It haunts me in the back of my mind like a phantom ghost, and it calls out in my spirit so callously, yet without reproach. This daunting, malicious unpredictable task that has somehow beckoned me to persevere in spite of the horrors that possibly could await me. **The prison cries: project.** You see, it's been a part of my young adult life which has transitioned to my middle-aged years and has continued to evolve during the life span of my career. This prison life of mine shuffles itself front and center with every aspect of my life. You see, yes, I do work in the prison, but, I cannot separate the fact that I am still serving time just as any other ward of the state. The only difference is that I elected to position myself as a public servant in the workplace with hopes to guide and transform the community via serving humanity from a therapeutic methodological standpoint from within. This apparatus was primarily designed to restore, enhance, repair, and restructure the brokenness of the individual within various segments of our inmate population. Most often, these are intensive training modules that augments an array of outstanding needs to make that individual that's incarcerated whole again. Upon being placed in the prison setting, some of the retraining aspects that are often explored are in the areas of educational/vocational training, welfare/social dynamics, mental health therapy, and cultural/spiritual living, etc. It is important to first help the young men in our prison community to strive toward achieving their goals in hopes to better prepare them for the future. It is certainly hoped that in order to matriculate back into mainstream society, the treatment programs will foster a renewed sense of hope that inspires self-determination through a wholistic point of view. The standard by which we garner this support is by any means necessary given the crucial task at hand. Ultimately, the goal is to make the individual whole again. Inherently, it is no doubt the case that the vast majority of young men in the Afro-American community are autodidact by nature. Consequently, in order to reclaim the formative years of our younger generation, many of which we are losing to the streets, we might need to consider revamping the whole childhood rearing process. We as a society from a wholistic point of view should consider whether or not every aspect of our community service system needs reform. We might need to hijack this train wreck and stage a military style coup d'état. The evidence for the case being made to weed out a cesspool of evil players, whether they are players with a criminal element on the side of law enforcement or within the prison community serving time is beside the point. Specifically, the criminal element within the confines of the prison walls will ultimately be our downfall, costing us two steps back for every one-step forward. There are so many alarming concerns that have crippled our criminal justice system. The United States has the largest population of incarcerated individuals in the world. There are approximately two million individuals currently serving time in the United States today according to the Bureau of Justice statistics. There still remains today a crucial recidivism rate which stands today on average an estimated 67% or three times the rate it was some thirty years ago. Our recidivism rate has tripled or in some cases quadrupled, given the targets for specific crimes (i.e., found within the scope of criminal profile data). The prison issues have taken the headlines of the day regarding all that can go wrong in our prison system. In the news today, May 21, 2012, it was reported from Tupelo, Mississippi, that authorities have now gained control of a twelve-hour riot that ended in one correctional officer being killed and several others seriously injured. Also, the United States Attorney's Office is looking into alleged civil right violations of women prisoners at Tutwiler prison for women located in Wetumpka, Alabama. The women are reporting allegations of sexual misconduct being committed by correctional staff at the prison. Reportedly, there have been numerous cases of sexual harassment, which has documented incidents that range from physical unwanted assaults to pregnancies that resulted from cases of rape. Most of these allegations were filed within the last five years. These are just a couple of articles about the horrid conditions found within our prison system. Then again, I am an eternal optimist, therefore, I expect great things. After years of still pushing on my journey, I have been truly blessed with an opportunity to meet so many people that have graciously allowed me to personally touch various intricate aspects of their lives. Surely, I have made many mistakes along the way, but, I would like to think that I have learnt from my egregious errors, and that today, I am a better person because of it. All my life I spent many years studying hard in school, to what seemed to me was a challenging sport to slam-dunk pop quizzes, score no hitters on major league tests, and secure the equivalent of Olympic gold executed on final exams, until finally I was blessed to graduate from college. Although it did prove to be a formidable task without a doubt, I made it through. In May of 1985, I received my Bachelor of Science degree in Administration of Criminal Justice from the University of North Carolina at Chapel Hill. I look to the hills from whence cometh my strength, my strength comes from the Lord. And I know that it was God that pulled me through college. And it's because of him that I am here today. Yet, and still, that degree only got me through my first benchmark. From there, I knew I needed to land a job. I knew that society carried certain prejudices that were prevalent in the '80s just as each generation is unique and has them associated with their own. And for the '80s, it was mainly being, inexperienced, being female and Afro-American that were targeted red flags specifically designed to narrow the scope of one's job search by insurmountable odds. Does some of this stuff sounds familiar? Déjà vu? Fast forward about twenty-some years and they still exist today. In spite of all that challenged me, my spirit remained hopeful. With me being the first in my family to receive a four year college degree, the expectations were high. I just couldn't let my family down. So I just couldn't give up no matter what. I knew I had to keep moving forward. And I made a promise to myself that I would someday return to college and pursue a graduate degree. But for now, I had to return to my childhood home from whence I came. That would be from a small town in Kinston, North Carolina. In a small apartment, low-income housing project was what I knew growing up as my home. After many, many months of struggling through the job hunt process, when I returned back home from college . . . life was so hard. I had no place to go back to except the only place I knew to call home. Now, if you approached this from an analytical standpoint, than, my situation with lodging had just suffered a setback. I had to return back to living with two roommates (i.e., my mom and my sister shared the same room with me) instead of the one roommate I had in college. For me, the Math didn't add up in my favor, it didn't seem at all like I was making any progress at this juncture. Not only that, my meager funds set aside in a savings account was a joke. Even though my pitiful prospects for gainful employment were low, my faith in God to lead the way was running on high. I only prayed that God bless soon and that the nightmare that I lived every day would somehow end. And I do truly thank God for answering prayers. I knew that the job hunt required at least nominal funds. I mean you need transportation and access to copy machines and printers to print resumes, computers to fax, scanners, telephones, etc. You also needed travel expenses, meals, and decent clothing as well. And these expenses could add up significantly on a budget with limited resources. Initially, trying to tackle the interviews for my early job prospects were nothing short of a nightmare. I stayed apprehensive about the whole process. I was horrified and extremely nervous as well. I felt that my wardrobe lacked the proper attire. I would often stumble over my responses, displayed limited eye contact, and repeatedly allowed my head to drop to the floor as well. Consequently, this would almost always crash any hope I had of gaining employment. Nevertheless, I practiced and rehearsed the techniques of role-play. Then, I launched my rebound. I worked hard every chance I got for an opportunity to secure gainful employment and hopefully launch my career. My efforts were making positive strides. There were so many leads that I had to follow-up with, although many were seemingly dubious at best. Yet, it remains a mystery to this day about the notion of how tracking letters played such a significant role in my job search. This letter campaign started out from an innocent and somewhat non-chalant stance, in efforts to appease my insatiable quest to gain employment. As previously stated, it began without much bang in theory, but, then serendipity ruled the order of the day. It soon gained traction and took off fast and fierce careening off the charts. Ultimately, it was through this letter writing campaign that my breakthrough landed a job. Now, my success did not come over night. It was a long hard fought battle before any victory came my way.

JOB SEARCH CAMPAIGN CHART:

DATE	POSITION	AGENCY	CONTACT/PERSON
MAY 1, 1985	JUVENILE JUSTICE COORDINATOR	CRIME CONTROL AND PULBIC SAFTY, NC	MR. JAMES R. SCARCELLA, DIRECTOR
JULY 29,1985	INTERVIEW	EXECUTIVE OPTIONS, INC MARKETING COMPANY, NJ	MS. JUDY FOX, ASSOCIATE PARTNER
JULY 30, 1985	PERSONNEL SPECIALIST TRAINEE	DEPARTMENT OF PUBLIC SAFETY& CORRECTIONAL SERV, MD	MS. ESTHER SCALION, PERSONNEL DIRECTOR
SEPT 15, 1985	PROBATION OFFICER	ADULT PROBATION & PAROLE, NC	MR. GEORGE RODISON, CONTROLLER
DEC 26, 1985	SOCIAL SERVICES ELIGIBILITY SPEC 1	GUILFORD COUNTY PERSONNEL DEPARTMENT, NC	MS. SHIRLEY ROSSON RECRUITMENT COORDINATOR
DEC 27, 1985	SOCIAL WORKER	OFFICE OF PERSONNEL MANAGEMENT, MD	MR. LLYOD BOWSER, AREA MANAGER
JAN 12, 1986	PROBATION COURT SERVICES OFFICER	ADMINISTRATIVE OFFICE OF ILLINOIS COURTS, IL	MR. R. BARRY BOLLENSEN, SUPERVISOR
JAN 23, 1986	**CORRECTIONAL OFFICER**	**D.C. OFFICE OF PERSONNEL WASHINGTON, D.C**	**MR. GLEN L BUCHANAN ASST. DIRECTOR OF PERSONNEL**
FEB 2, 1986	PROBATION OFFICER INTERVIEW	DEPARTMENT OF JUSTICE RALEIGH, NORTH CAROLINA	MR. GEORGE ROBISON III, CONTROLLER
FEB 20, 1986	ADULT PROBATION OFFICER	CIRCUIT COURT OF COOK COUNTY, CHICAGO, ILLINOIS	MR. THOMAS CUNNINGHAM, EXECUTIVE OFFICER
MAR 5, 1986	PROBATION OFFICER	DEPARTMENT OF PROBATION AND COURT SERVICES, WHEATON, ILL	MS. NANCY SUTHERLAND ADMINISTRATIVE SEC
MAR 8, 1986	ADULT PROBATION OFFICER	CIRCUIT COURT OF COOK COUNTY, CHICAGO, ILLINOIS	MR. RICHARD NAPOLI, CHIEF PROBATION OFFICER
JAN 2, 1987	**CORRECTIONAL TREATMENT SPECIALIST**	**D.C. OFFICE OF PERSONNEL WASHINGTON, D.C.**	**MR. MEL JACKSON, PERSONNEL REPRESENTATIVE**
OCT 2, 1995	SUPERVISOR CORRECTIONAL TREATMENT SPEC	D.C. OFFICE OF PERSONNEL WASHINGTON, N.C.	MS. CLAUDIA LANCASTER, PERSONNEL REPRESENTATIVE
JAN 3, 2003	HEARING EXAMINER D.C. PAROLE BOARD	D.C. OFFICE OF PERSONNELL WASHINGTON, D.C.	MS. PATRICIA JACKSON, PERSONNEL REPRESENTATIVE

The correspondence incurred from my job search letters would usually end with something like the following: Thank you, but this position has already been filled. We will keep your application on file. We appreciate your interest and wish you the best of luck in your job search. Needless to say, whenever I received letters that contained any of the correspondence cited above, I knew instinctively that there would be no further contact from that particular agency. In all honesty, the job search process can be a tremendous drain on your energy sources both mentally and physically. Quite frankly, in order to replenish your energy, sometimes you have to step back and take a break. But just don't quit. Hence, despite your present circumstances, you have to remember that the job search market is a fiercely competitive process that often demands that you to be versatile whenever possible. Furthermore, it has often been said that desperate times calls for desperate measures. Well, with respect to the job search market, this is indeed the gospel truth on so many levels.

It was my lifelong dream to venture out on my own and experience the real world. I was ambivalent about where I found myself which was in the jaws of a skittish job market on the heels of a petulant recession. Yet, somehow, I was frankly, pleasantly surprised by modest glimmers of hope. Then, after many days stewing over my thoughts of depression and drowning my troubles in despair, I ventured over to the court house one day, where at the time, I ran into a girl, solely by happenstance, who was around my same age, scavenging the job list, scrolling through possibilities, while scoping out the job openings. I remember seeing her from time to time at my high school, yet we never had a class together. She had always appeared quiet, reserved, and kept to herself. Yet, she lived around the same neighborhood which we all knew to be Richard Green or Carver Courts. As a matter of fact, I remember seeing her often walking to school as well. I can never forget the long walks home to and from school. That experience was just a nightmare for me. You see, we grew up in a low-income housing project, and just the environment itself, that particular culture is germane to breeding tribal wars. If you lived in a certain low-income project which is due to no fault of your own, by the way, it's simply where your parents found housing. Unfortunately, you are defined by that location. In fact, that location became your identity right along with everybody that lived there. If your location had a lot of thieves, robbers, number runners, liquor houses, thugs, drug dealers, crack heads, etc., than that was who you were declared to be as well. You were not allowed to dream about defying the odds. In others words, you were not expected to do above or beyond that specific standard or lifestyle that was established in that neighborhood. Now, if you thought of yourself as being different or perhaps dreams or goals different from the neighborhood from whence you came, then you had to prove it. If you had goals or aspirations to be better than the people that presumably defined your future, than you were frown upon. Immediately, from that point to on, you were forced to comply with the standards of the location from which you came. To do otherwise would cause you to be labeled a rebel or an outsider. From there, you were always the target of a fight. The truth be told the hood was never short on groups of girls ganging-up on one another to settle scores. The truth be told, most hood girls always brought attitude, just 'cause they would diss (i.e., meaning to disrespect) one another at the blink of an eye and they loved drama. Most girls wanted to fight over small scores that won't about nothing. In most cases, for me personally, I would say that the conflict centered on the area of low self-esteem. I also personally believed that there were issues which had deep-seated resentment toward authority as well. So there was always a tinderbox waiting to exploded. You see, whenever authority lacks the right combination of respect, the situation gets out of hand. It's very delicate because from time to time that same formula could deviated depending on the circumstances. Obviously, the girls felt they had to prove their self-worth and the choice that was made to get the adulation that they were seeking was by fighting. So fighting served as a catalyst by which they established a reputation for themselves. The street fight got respect for this type of notoriety, although truly misguided brought a false sense of pride as well. It is very important that young people learn to define who they are for themselves and not let others define for them who they are. And many of these issues dealing with self-esteem begin at home. Okay, at the end of the day, yeah, you accomplished popularity, respect and a reputation, but all for the wrong reasons. The majority of the girls from my neighborhood, they wanted to be bullies, and craved popularity. These girls in the so-called hood fought over anything. They have fought over boys, girls, money, cars, new shoes, new hats, new coats, new jackets, news dress, clothes, jewelry, etc. Now, as previously mentioned, most of this maladaptive behavior could have been addressed by the parents at home. But the parents either were not there or simply did not care. Unfortunately, in most cases, the parents were not mature enough to deal with the task of raising kids themselves. Now, in my own particular case, I was readily labeled a target because I never associated myself with who they were. They, being the people in my neighborhood. I was basically a loner. I functioned well on my own. I was self-contained, and I didn't need a crowd. I do remember walking to school with the neighborhood kids from my housing project. And from where we lived in Richard Green Apartments which was right down the street from Craver Courts, we walked to and from school together. I knew that certain kids in Carver Courts, and some right there in Richard Green, for that matter didn't like me.

For some reason, they always wanted to fight me, even though I never understood exactly why that was the case. And I still to this day never understood the root cause or the genesis of such a preposterous roust. All I do know is that I never liked their company, and we had nothing in common. I can recall one hot summer day walking home from school. Just as sweat was pouring down each eye-brow, the palms of both my hands grew clammy and wet. From the sound of the big wild bully, Mackenzie Franks, she was targeting her remarks toward me. Her remarks were, "I will beat the shit out our black ass today, 'cause yow black ass is all mine." I thought to myself, oh my god, what is she about to do? Why is she cussing at me for? She setup comments to target a fight with me. Everyone wanted to see her fight, they just didn't want to be the target of ill reproof. I could hear the remarks that she made as they became louder and louder. Beckoning me to heed her call to square off and start to fight. I could hear a small crowd around me chanting as I began to speed up my pace to sweaty armpits and weak wobbly knees. As the crowd kept shouting "fight, fight, fight," I felt my blood in my body boil, I was hot all over. Then, my feet got stiff and nervous. At some point, my heart left my chest and it settled in my throat. My eyes whelm up with a tusanmina of tears, and my cheeks exploded up high, swollen from feverishly rubbing teardrops that sped down my face. I tried but couldn't stop the tears. The crowd laughed at me and yet cheered the bully on. I sped up my pace to try to avoid the confrontation. I used my mind to eclipse the loud voices around me, which plummeted me with insults at every hand. I meditated on silence. The silence that I came to know whenever the lowest point of my world reined supreme in my life. At the point of eclipse, the silence once again became my refuge. The silence insulated me from the cruel, filth and garbage that reeked from this bully's foul mouth. From there, I was able to stop the reeling of my out of control bodily functions and regain my composure. The silence helped me to control my nerves and calmed my fears. At some point, the tears stopped, shortly after that, my clumsy, fast pace trot came to a screeching halt. At the drop of a dime, I threw both hands up in the air, and lunged forward, starring wild eyed at the bully who was (obviously caught off guard) startled, and she jumped back in her tracks. She, then took off running in the opposite direction, as if her breeches were on fire, I mean you would have thought that she had seen a ghost. Since, that day, I never encountered that bully again. She would never cross my path again and that was just the way I liked it. I never could have known what would have happened, had she not ran, I'm just so glad she did. To this day, I have attributed the events of that day as an act of god, for which I know of there being no other possible explanation.

Well, besides the bully, there were several other classmates while growing up that I do remember. As I mentioned earlier, there was this one girl in particular whom I later found out was named Joann. Now, as far back as I could recall, we really never spoke or had conversations besides just random eye-balling one another, yet, nothing beyond keeping private, nursing our fleeting thoughts as they would often times vividly dissolve . . . disappeared as quickly as they injected themselves on the scene. As years went by, we just kept our life affairs going without having any legitimate reason to have our worlds intertwine. In other words, our paths never crossed, at least, not until that moment. So we both managed to mutter an awkward, bashful, dreadful noise that perhaps masked the muffled sound of a *"Hello"*. (Spoken in Eskimo language). From that moment on, our words easily flowed. In fact, our conversation jet skidded off without a hitch, almost like one of Thomas's steam engine trains. Now, on that particular day, we were both hot and tired after an early start on our job search. Unfortunately, neither one of us had had any luck that day. As we both stood in the lobby of Lenoir County Court house in Kinston, we stood there with great anticipations. We browsed through the job opening rack, as if pirates hunting for buried treasure. It was there, when I asked her what jobs was she looking for. She replied, "Aweeeee hello, I'm Joann, I've seen you before." "Oh yeah," I quickly responded. "I'm Carleen, I remember seeing you too at Kinston High School, right." So, we exchanged familiar pleasantries about our neighborhoods. As we both walked and talked we approached the corridor equipped with table and chairs. After being seated at the table, we both shared more of our concerns. Then, Joann pivoted the conversation back to the job search. "I'm trying to find a position in adult parole supervision or the juvenile family court system. I recently graduated from Fayetteville State University with a BS in Criminal Justice and Psychology. I've been back home since May of last year, which will be fifteen months in August. So, after spending all that time looking for work, I still have not found a job." Then, I thought to myself, I'm really not alone out here dealing with this. Somebody else understands my struggle. So, I explained, "I just recently graduated as well. I haven't had any luck either. And, lately, I've been thinking . . . Is this how it's suppose to be?" I mean I've spent almost nineteen years of my life, studying hard, playing by all the rules, waiting for my turn to lay the right foundation. I guess what I'm trying to say is that I went to high school and earned a diploma. From there, I was blessed to go to college and fulfill the American dream. And, by the grace of God, I did graduate and received my diploma. Now, I desperately need a job. And the workforce is so cruel, condescending, and disingenuous that it can often make one feel unwanted, disenchanted, or inadequate, when all you really want is a chance to prove your self-worth." And, after letting all of that explode, I slowly exhaled and automatically, fired off another diatribe. "All I can think about right now is that my whole life I spent most of my time trying to do what's right and play by the rules, just to be treated like a common criminal. What I'm saying is that not one job interview turned out to be in my favor. I mean, I go to the interview thinking that all I needed is at least the minimal requirements, which is no doubt a four year degree, but, then I learnt that it's all about who you know, and the degree is irreverent. Carleen then concluded her remarks by saying, "I really hope to God I can leave here someday." After listening to Carleen's expose, Joann shared her problem. "I received a job offer in the mail from Washington, D.C. A couple of days ago, but, I can't go anywhere right now with my mother being so sick. I really need to stay close to home." Joann continued in a desperate tone. "You see, I'm the oldest of two. See, my siblings are twelve and fifteen and, if I want my mom cared for properly, than I will have to see to it myself." Then, she said, "As a matter fact, I am not in the position to move away to take that job right now. I need to be right here close to home because of my mom's sickness. She needs me and she has always been there for me, so I won't leave her at a time that she needs me most." She then hung her head in sadness. Well, I can truly understand that. But then Carleen leaned back in her chair with a twinkle in both eyes. Almost instantly, she had a brilliant idea. Carleen was notified that she was selected for a position with court services in Kinston, Lenoir County. This news came as she checked her emails for updates. Then, Carleen spoke brisk and sharp. "Hey, Joann, I have an idea. Why don't you take my job here in Kinston, and I take your job offer in Washington, D.C? Joann began to lift up her head, clap both hands, and slowly nodded to express her approval. After working out the logistics that involved compliance with protocol, that's exactly what they did. She took my job and I took hers.

I don't believe for one moment that no one is up there watching over the utter chaos that's going on down here on earth. You cannot convince me that there is no gatekeeper minding the storehouse. God is in control of all that we hear, do, or say. He is the alpha, and omega. He is the great I am. So, don't try to tell me that my God is not in control. This world does seem crazy sometimes. And definitely nowadays more often times than not. You see, because I don't have the mind of God, there is so much that I will never be able to understand. Even in my particular case, I arrived here just like everybody else on the scene, yet, given a unique set of circumstances, none of which I selected or chose. The mere fact that we as a human race exist on the planet is an act of God. I was born to my mother out of wedlock. She was twenty-nine years old when I was born. My mother came from a large family. She had ten brothers and sisters and she was the youngest. She lost her own mom when she was a teenager herself. She was fourteen years old when her mom passed away. Then, shortly after that, a couple years later, she lost her dad too. So at sixteen years old, she was virtually left to figure out the world that she lived in on her own. Most of us would agree likewise that life can often be complicated for adults, let alone a child. Yet, and still, she had to somehow get through childhood, puberty, and adulthood all on her own. But thank God, she had one sister, Aunt Mary who took her in and helped raised her. She has stayed with Aunt Mary all her life. And it was Aunt Mary who helped raise all of us as well. I am the youngest of four girls being raised by a single low income seasonal farm worker. Our first house was a big old wood three-story house. It was this house that was shared by me, my mom, my aunt, and my three sisters. I can still remember the day that we had to vacate the property on Harvey Street due to a fire that burned our house down. The fire department condemned the property because the house burnt to the ground. The fire department said that the cause of the fire was undetermined. All I know is that this was one of the saddest days of my life. The fire destroyed everything we had. On the day of the fire, no one was at home, thank god. We had headed out early on that particular morning to church. My aunt Mary had left before we all got up and went to work. She was what was called a service worker for the mayor, Mr. Sterling Grant. He was one of Kinston's most prominent, charismatic statesmen. He was very kind to Aunt Mary and she worked for almost thirty years. She enjoyed her job and she did finally retire after being racked with bad health problems: high blood pressure and sugar diabetes, yet, her final blow was experiencing the onset of her primary health flaw, arthritis. In fact, she suffered from acute arthritis. So at about sixty-seven years old, her medical problems basically ended her career. Aunt Mary was married briefly but that never worked out and it ended in divorce. She had no children born to this union. For the record, Aunt Mary never had any children. So she helped raised all of us as her own. After the big fire at our house on Harvey Street, we moved to the projects. Now, being caught in transitional stages for low-income housing with four young kids can be frightening. Yet, what made the experience more surreal were several nights spent in a homeless shelter, waiting for our new apartment to open in the projects. In hindsight, we all agreed that spending that weekend at the shelter for the homeless was a stern lesson in humility that enriched our lives . . . time and time again. And, despite being overwhelmed with ambivalence, we got ready for bed early both nights, desperately clinging to every glimmer of hope that our new apartment would be ready come Monday morning. And, finally, our prayers were answered, late Monday evening, social services delivered the keys to our new apartment at 200 East Bright street. From the depths of pain and despair to the victory snatched from the jaws of defeat, we gave God the glory. Now, on the following Tuesday morning, my mother and aunt Mary went to the Richard Green Apartments and opened the door with that new key. At that point, we were no longer homeless. We had succinctly made the move from Harvey Street into a three-bedroom apartment in another part of town. It took about two weeks to get the emergency public assistance program for low-income housing to be approved by the Department of Social Services. From there, we lived on public assistance for as long as I could remember. For years, the sole source of income was from Aunt Mary 'cause my mom worked as a day-laborer, often on the farms. She would rise early mornings (approximately 5:00 a.m.), along with fifteen to twenty workers and catch a big old school bus, or some old raggedy halfbroke down truck to go off to a farm for a day's labor to crop tobacco, pick blue berries, string beans, or sweet potatoes. And at sun down, they would always return home with daily wages (approximately $20.00-$25.00 cash money). We were thankful for the pay, she got to buy the food to put a meal on the table (enough for a few days). Nevertheless, as the summer months began to fade and fall eased her way into the fabric of our lives, the day labor truck no longer etched its way to the curb alongside bright street to pick up the laborers to work the fields. All the crops had been harvested and seeds planted for next summer, just as the onset of seasonal changes of fall and winter sprung into action, which generated a brief pause of anticipation, from routine daily chores, and we improvised. We all lived together under one roof as a family, being raised with Aunt Mary and our mom. During the early years of her youth, our mom was a smart worker. Although she didn't have any formal education, she always told us that we had to go to college no matter what. She knew that she couldn't afford one penny to send us off to a college, but, she would always say study hard and God will make a way. All throughout her youth. She was a worker. She worked hard every day now. I was never that close to my mother, in fact, she really didn't come across as being that close to anyone. I have never in my lifetime heard her say anything good about us. She has never spoken the words "I love you" to either of us. But she knew how to cuss us out.

From that experience, I learnt how to behave with reverence and respect in hopes to avoid the trashing of a sharp, disdainful, callous tongue. In fact, one of the few times that she spoke to us was when it was about something that we did wrong. And most of the time that we got into trouble, was when we decided for whatever reason chose to be disobedient. In other words, we actually were defiant and elected to break the rules. Now, in most cases these rules were to be home at night on time and no staying out past midnight, no boys allowed for dating (no exceptions), and finally no playing around in school, and school work ranks number one on chores without exceptions. Then, last but not least, Sunday school and church on Sundays were mandatory. Now, if you got caught violating these rules, whereby you were rarely ever granted reprieve than your head was on the chopping block and you got served. And that's when we got a whooping and a good cussing out. With that being said, as I look back on my upbringing as child, I believe that my mom truly loved us, she just didn't want us to make the same mistakes that she did. I also learnt something else about my mother growing up, which was that she thought very highly of herself. I would often catch her in the mirror, combing her hair or putting on lipstick. And she was an attractive woman. She had always attributed her looks to her good genes that she took after her mom, but, her long hours spent being meticulously well-groomed didn't hurt either. In her mind, her looks were paramount to her livelihood and bartered on her self-esteem. As the years went by, she was hard pressed to comes to grips with the fact that balancing both the beauty and glee of one's youth mounts a ubiquitously challenging task when you are faced with the burden of growing old and losing the youthful days of pride and glee. Growing older in a brutal harsh, cold and dubious world that we live in today brings unnecessary extra hardship in our lives. It is also significant to note that my mom lost her mother at a young age. Therefore, being without the guidance of an adult to play a prominent role in her life. She had no one to explain to her about the onset of puberty, about the odious and contemptuous malicious, well-guarded and often wayward young men that talked young girls into sex before they marry (sexual perverted acts). Now, falling prey to these choices would guarantee a poor, young, black girl a life time of poverty that perpetuates itself seven times seven for seventy years of servitude constituting a curse to the family bloodline for generations to come. This was an old timey folklore in black culture with biblical ties (Lev. 26:21). There was no one that took the time to explain to her how to protect herself from being compromised by the use of alcohol, drugs, illicit behaviors that leads to a dead end. And no adult explained to her about how important it was for young black men and women to get a good education. God knows that when he created man that he made him intelligent. He knows that you have the good common sense that he gave you and that you should choose obedience. So follow God's laws and be blessed and highly favored in the land. Also, life itself, if left alone without guidance and discipline, it will get worst. In fact, poverty is the worst curse on earth. It is significant to note that heathens beget heathens and this curse is then passed on from generation to generation. As previously stated, there was no one to explain how important it was to stay in school, get an education, respect your body, and love yourself first before thinking about getting involved with someone else. In other words, teach our youth not to perpetuate the curse of poverty from generation to generation, but choose obedience, follow God's laws, and prosper in the land. Unfortunately, my mom, she grew up without either parent to give her instructions about life. Now, by us living with Aunt Mary, my mom was often scolded by Aunt Mary about what was right and wrong, but, for the most part, she was left to pursue her own devices. She had no road map. She didn't have a clue. Now, my dad, I often thought of him within the context of a cliché—you can't miss what you never had. But, you know what, I painfully missed what I never did get to have. I longed for a dad, and thought for the better part of all my youth or until my dad was killed that if I was good enough that I would someday get to have a dad. And if not my own dad, then somebody else's. Well, it goes without saying that the mystery of the human mind has never ceased to amaze me. As I sit alone in my room and I scream at the vicious emotional brutality of my situation. But no sound is released. There is only silence. Silence at my frustrations. And, in my mind, there is a silence so loud, that my voice could be heard at the top of Mount Kilimanjaro. It is amazing how fluid the thoughts of the mind can ebb and flow from the manufacturing one constant epoch of life's transformations to another. Yet, still, others around you would never catch a glimpse of the hydraulics that fuel the mind. All these thoughts can be calibrated from one split second to the next. And quite often this is what happens in real time. These fleeting thoughts that bask within a shroud of glowing mystiques, they energize the mind, hence, balancing one's sense of reality. What a powerful instruments that we as humans have been blessed by God to have, when God equipped us with the mind. It is the most marvelous creation ever made. It is phenomenal, yet, not daunted by all its folly. The dynamics of the human mind are forever evolving. At times, it can be as giddy as a schoolboy, or as crass and bold as a tart root beer float that capitulates a brain freeze at the drop of a dime. I have often wondered why my family was in such a dire strait situation financially, and what brought all of this about. What constituted the plight of our lifestyle and why can't we do better? Well, many of these answers never came about until I was much older. During my childhood, I experienced many nights going to bed hungry without a meal. In fact, we almost never got a breakfast before school, nor a desert after mealtime. Lord knows we never got a dessert. I mean I thought, as a child, that at mealtime, if I was on my best behavior, then why couldn't I have a desert? I mean besides being hungry, we had scarce household amenities. So, given the fact that we were scrapped for cash, we just couldn't afford a dessert. Often, the choice between buying clothes and shoes was secondary to the prospects of preparing a halfway decent meal, let alone a dessert. The house fire resulted in the lost of everything we ever had. Aunt Mary would bring us home boxes of old clothes and shoes that Mr. Sterling Grant's family threw away. So, we used all that we could to survive from one day to the next. We also used social services, or better known as the government welfare/ food stamp system 'cause there was not enough food. There were times growing up. I would try to think of my dad and what he was really like or who he really was. And what it would really be like to have a father in the household. We never knew anything about him other than what our mom told *us*. Well, one day we got word that my dad was killed, shot dead in New York by his lover. It was an extremely difficult time for my mom. She loved him very much and always spoke great things about him. I believe that she spent her life telling herself that he would someday come home. She never dated anyone else and never moved on. She just wanted this one man, the father of her children to come back home to help her raise her girls. Now, he was dead and that would never happen. I felt more sadness for her than the thought of him being dead. In fact, I felt nothing for him, I had only seen him twice in my lifetime. Once when I was about seven years old and the second time was when I attended his funeral. And, to be truly honest, I didn't want to go. There are many thoughts that come to my mind when I think of his death. So I wrote a poem about how it intrigued me and how very often it troubled me. A poem that I called "On the other side: on the other side."

What do people do there on the other side?

Is it cold or rainy or just summertime all day on the other side? Do people comfort one another during times of despair? Where do they go during times of joy? How do they fine peace? Are they all suffering hopelessly within . . . or locked away seeking the untold mysteries? This we will never know while present here on earth. We just know that we will meet them again soon someday in another part of the universe. On the other side someday, we'll know all these answers—death will no longer drape or hide its jaded face . . . for we all must enter unto his glory. For God has made for all mankind his own resting place—on the other side. Godspeed!

I have not always been able to think good thoughts about my dad, but, I have made great strides toward the concept of forgiveness. And I know I have a long way to go, but I'm still evolving to a higher self. So, this is what I aspire to be every day. See, life is too short. I have just one chance to get it right. I just don't want to miss it. And my dad has already answered his call to glory. There is nothing left in this earth for any of us to do for him. The best that we can do now is learn all we can from those that went before us and be better in this life than those that ventured on to glory behind us.

Specifically, times have not drastically changed regarding mainstream public views about women . . . as previously mention. It's been strikingly evident that the headline news these days is all about the Republicans and their all out assault on women's rights. A very recent article in the news was about Sandra Fluke, a young lady Georgetown University law student, who testified before congress about Georgetown University's policy on contraceptives on February 23, 2012. The issue at hand was that Georgetown did not cover contraceptive services for female students in their policy. These hearings drew a plethora of criticisms from political pundits. In fact, Rush Limbaugh, talk show host, was lethal and cut throat in his incideniary remarks. He called her a slut and a whore. He said that the only way that the taxpayers should cover her contraceptives was that we the public be allowed to watch her sex acts on tape. The remarks made on his radio show about Sandra Fluke prompted a telephone call from President Barack Obama, whereby, he apologized on national television for the remarks made by the talk show host. In closing, he told her that her parents should be proud of her. Also, there was the Lilly Ledbetter equal pay act of 2009, which required equal pay for women in the work force, yet, these measures were defeated on May 21, 2012 in the house of representatives. This act amends Title VII by affording women the right to pursue a remedy for paycheck discrimination under antidiscrimination laws. And on June 5, 2012, Senator Barbra Mikulski brought the Paycheck Fairness Act before the senate, but it failed to advance by a vote of 52-47, falling short of the sixty vote threshold needed to break a filibuster. Also, the violence against women act was initially defeated in the House of Representatives on May 21, 2012, but it was revisited and passed on February 12, 2013. The passage of this law would protect women's rights against violence and discrimination. Although these are current news headlines of today, the ubiquitous chain of events are evidence of just how little our status quo has changed for women's rights, therefore, indicative of how so much has remained the same.

Now, my job seeking adventure has literally been an adventure. On one of my interviews, there was an opportunity for me to get hired as a juvenile justice coordinator. Nevertheless, a whistle blower alerted me by happenstance that the position had already been promised to a co-worker's family member. This family member supposedly already worked for the state. In my opinion, the interview went fine. But I knew something was wrong when allegedly a fake applicant kept interrupting the interview with fresh coffee, napkins, and token items such as: note pads, Sharpee pens, and shotgun folders, etc. These workers were all spear heading this rude behavior. By the third time she made her entrance, (supposedly this family member), there was no need to continue with the interview. That whole setup was crass. Furthermore, Mr. Lemon, Asst. Director of Personnel never corrected the situation. When I finished the last question of the interview, I felt like the third man out in a game of musical chairs. I did thank Mr. Lemon for his time and promptly left. I just wanted to get out of there and forget that whole scene. I wanted to start fresh and move on. I don't think that that situation would have been a healthy environment for me anyway. And I welcomed the idea of looking elsewhere. So, I did.

First of all, I was not aware of all the turmoil that faced the Lorton Prison Complex prior to being hired to work there. I needed a job desperately and I was just ecstatic about finally being given the opportunity to launch my career. So, yes, you can say that I delved into the contract with blinders on. This was at a point in my life that I felt that taking that job was the right thing to do. It was good news that I could finally tell my family instead of the news of another rejection. In hindsight, I probably would have made the same choice in spite of the fact that all the cards were not stacked in my favor (i.e., forthcoming the Lorton closure). I have always leaned on God to work it all out at the end of the day. In fact, while growing up in the projects, my mother always taught us that if we did our best then God would always step in and do the rest. And from all of my experiences, thus far, this had always proven to be true. Nevertheless, upon being hired, on February 2, 1986, as a correctional officer, I was subsequently enrolled in the Lorton Training Academy. From there, I made every effort to satisfy all task on every hand to the extent that I accomplished my goals with hard work and determination. At the end of the day, I was able to satisfy the requirements for the completion of the Lorton Training Academy. It is significant to note that I received my completion on the heels of a brief ceremony, March 7, 1986, along with twenty-nine to thirty classmates held at the Lorton Training Academy. The ceremony itself lasted for approximately forty to forty-five minutes. In attendance at the ceremony which acknowledged our hard work and determination was the director of the department of corrections, Mr. John Ridley, Training Academy administrator, Mr. William Beck, and training instructor, Ms. Veeni Overia. In addition, there were others (i.e., wardens, supervisors, lieutenants, sergeants, etc.) who were assigned to various facilities that were in attendance as well. Shortly after graduation, we were assigned to a duty station and expected to report for work at the close of businesses day. Upon acquiring this newfound status, we now had to stand on our own and confront the odious task of surviving correctional officer rookie class 101. Technically, we not only had to talk the talk, but we now had to walk the walk too. This would be considered on-the-job training, which allows the rookie correctional officer to be exposed to the formidable task of surviving inmate con-games 101 at the Lorton Complex. Now, the overall performance of one's duties would make or break the rookie at the end of the day. So, vetted with brand new officers on the front line for duty, a new chapter was about to sweep in the catalyst for which change at the Lorton Complex would begin it's reign. Nevertheless, be advised that there were other nefarious aspects of the Lorton Complex that waged a covert warfare under the radar of mundane events disguised as routine protocol. In hindsight, the prison operated from the mindset of business as usual. However, in reality behind the scenes, the Lorton Complex was just a powder keg waiting to explode, yet, there were no visible signs that yielded warnings on display. Nevertheless, the sheer thought of making an entrance into the facility caused me to shudder. Once the gate sled open to allow passage, you could not erase the sounds projected from the eminence of brazen, sharp, click-clacks-clunks (i.e., gates in operation) that deafens the brinks of sound. Next, anxiety instantly floods the mind. Can you imagine being captured like a trapped mouse, between two sliding tall fences, hedged with reams of razor barbed wire, which are opened (sliding left and right) by a mechanical locking device? All of which are operated by guards in a tower, high above a brick wall of the fenced razor barbed wire. The heart rate pumps fast in anticipation of the gate being opened to allow you to proceed into the entrance. Finally, a sigh of relief beams across the flesh and anxiety seems to fade when released from between the two sliding gates, hence, ultimately gaining access. After being allowed to proceed through the gates, you enter through a large cement door. At that point, the search of all your personal property begins. This routine operational procedure was standard protocol, yet, it was almost never met without contempt. Not to mention the dubious consternation of the staff that operated that particular post. If closely tracking the Lorton train wreck snafu, one might have taken notice of news reports on the wire which chastised the management staff at Lorton for an array of mishaps, for which many suffered disdain and scorn. Yet, and still, much of the public was not aware of Lorton's deplorable conditions nor the nefarious liabilities causing it to be sanctioned by federal courts. Although later I became aware of the Lorton Complex being put under court order monitoring by federal judge June Greene for eons of egregious foul behaviors which could not be tolerated or ignored within the scope of any prison setting. These findings got the Occoquan facility at Lorton on the map for being known as "the district's most violent prison" which by the way is located the on the east coast. This report was by Locy, Toni, and Vise, David? in a article from the newspaper in the Washington Post, December, 6, 1995, vol. 119 issue 1. Pd1. There were numerous of live news streams, documented accounts of media reporting on conditions of gang fights, inmate stabbings, murders, assaults, robberies, drug trafficking (crack and heroin networks), sexual assaults, escapes, etc. All of the above violated the law, yet, at the same time these criminal acts were the inmates' code of conduct by which they governed themselves. In fact, this type of criminal conduct was considered as standard operational procedures held within the confines of the Lorton Complex. In addition to all of these concerns, the Lorton Complex was plagued by severe overcrowding, limited resources and staff shortages. It is significant to note that the Lorton Complex was made up of at least seven to ten facilities. In addition, it should be noted that although the actual count of the structural sites were seven, there were facilities in which the population count was large enough to have separate camps within one facility. And Occoquan was one such facility at Lorton which had a large enough population to establish three camps that operated within the same facility. That was why the Occoquan facility was referred to by all in the workplace and throughout the Lorton Complex as Occoquan zone i, zone ii and zone iii. In addition, it was often referred to as the "quack." This was primarily because of the sheer bizarre nature from which the pandering monopolized. It was essentially an anomaly within its own right. For example, it seemed profoundly strange to me how that inmates could always manage to get their voices heard without having to go through a chain-of-command, or address formalities, whereas, on the other hand, all staff had to address formal protocol in order to get their concerns addressed on any level, hence came the term "quack." The story of the Lorton reformatory began with the D.C. Government entering into a contact for the purchase of land from Virginia for $1.00 (1700-1800+ per square acres) for one hundred years. Then, the Lorton Complex opened in 1910 by the federal government as a rehabilitation camp for district convicts. It was said to be needed because the district had no space for which to build a prison nor to house detainees (i.e., specifically women) for processing upon being taken into custody. So in order to address the need for separate quarters for women once detained and processed by D.C. Police, many women were taken down to Lorton. During much of the early 1900s Washington, D.C. Was the center stage for women marching for women's suffrage. Many women marched the streets of the nation's capital for the right to vote and to have equal rights under the laws that had been afforded to men. When they were arrested for marching without a permit, they were sent down to Lorton or to what was known as a work camp. They were held there for processing. And upon completion, they were subsequently released. From there, the camp expanded over the years and grew by leaps and bounds. Then, reportedly between 1916-1920s, construction of multiple facilities began in efforts to handle the over crowding from the detainees at the D.C. Jail. Shortly after that, women were removed all together from the Lorton reformatory and transferred out to contract facilities or to surrounding counties preferably in West, Virginia (Alderson federal prison, 1927). At some point, by the mid 1980s and 1990s, the Lorton Complex held approximately seven (7-10) facilities. The Lorton Complex has held approximately 10, 000+ inmates when it was operational at full capacity. The name(s) of the facilities are listed as follows: Medium Facility, Youth Center, Occoquan Facility, Minimum Security Facility, Modular Facility, Maximum Security Facility, and Central Facility.

Lorton Complex

Facility	Custody level	Sentence	Profile status
Occoquan i, ii, iii	Med	5 yrs > ped	Sentenced felon
Medium	Med	5 yres< ped or std	Sentenced felon
Youth center i, ii	Med	2 yrs < ped/5 yrs std	Court ordered yra
Central facility	Med/high	15-20 yrs > ped	Sentenced felon
Modular	Low/med	2yrs > 10	Court diagnostics
Maximum	High	20-life	Sentenced felon
Minimum security	Min	24 months < ped	Sentenced felon

As I previously stated, my career with the D.C. Department of Corrections began in February 1986. Consequently, I was on duty during the prison disturbance at the Occoquan facility at Lorton. The incident took place on July 10, 1986. I reported to work at approximately 11:00 p.m. for the midnight shift where I was assigned to the adjustment unit. This particular unit housed inmates designated as protective custody, special handling, disciplinary and/or administrative transfers, escape risk, etc. The melee began when inmates started fires in there housing units. In hindsight, it became obvious that the whole incident was planned because the fires set off a chain reaction that sparked a series of small fires being set through the whole compound. The quick pace of the rapid blazing fires became difficult to manage with limited staff being deployed to various locations. Nevertheless, because of the outstanding correctional skills demonstrated by the officers assigned to the adjustment unit, we were able to maintain control while literally under seize (i.e., prison takeover). We kept control of that entire cellblock until being forced to evacuate because of fire. The fire that we encountered was set by inmates who climbed on the roof of our building. We controlled the entire cellblock which contained some of the most hostile and violent inmates at Lorton. Yet, we did not have a fire set by any inmate contained in that cellblock. We were all commended for hard work, dedication, and a job well done on that night shift during the disturbance. In order to regain control of the institution, surrounding counties (Fairfax, Alexandria, and Suffolk) had to send reinforcement. Most of the buildings at the Occoquan facility had to be rebuilt (approximately fourteen out of twenty-four buildings burned to the ground). Reportedly, the riot resulted in the death of one young man, nineteen years old. He died due to a hell fire storm of rubber pellets being sprayed by law enforcement, while he lied in submission on the ball field. His death was essentially due to a lack of medical attention or more specifically their lack of response in a timely manner. After the police shot a hell firestorm of pellets, they were afraid to enter the facility due to fear for their own safety. Hence, they feared for the safety of medical personnel, the ambulance and/or EMS teams as well. So, as previously mentioned, in certain cases medical attention was either delayed and/or not administered in a timely manner. There were scores of other inmates and some staff injured as well. After clearer heads prevailed, in the mist of the crisis, emergency personnel were allowed on the scene. At some point, the feds agreed to house some of the district's inmates. Shortly after that, D.C. Shipped about 500 inmates to the feds. In the interim, random federal transfers were scheduled biweekly, per an emergency executive order for D.C. Department of corrections by the federal bureau of prisons. From there, many other transfers followed as well. A short time later, I was promoted to the position of correctional treatment specialist. However, I still remained assigned to the Occoquan facility.

Today, began slow and lethargic. As a matter of fact, I almost could not keep up pace with the time of the day. You see, all I wanted to do was to get home as fast as I could, fix a hot plate, and try to settle down so that I could get some rest. Nevertheless, I felt that it was time to contemplate the agenda for the next day. There were so many thoughts about the closure at Lorton that I just didn't know where to begin. Quite frankly, first and foremost, what comes to mind is finding another job. I had been at Lorton so long (since 1986) and that's where I wanted to stay until I retired. Even though I had heard from time to time about the closure of Lorton it really was more or less surreal to me. I really just chalked it up as rumors. It was a Lorton pastime and apart of Lorton's culture to exploit certain aspects of truth, pontificate and spread hearsay, and lies. Shortly after coming to work at Lorton in February 1986, it was usually mentioned in conversations with co-workers that Lorton would be closing in about ten years from now. But, at that time, I just needed a job and the thought of Lorton closing was the furthest thing from my mind. You see, the rumors would start out with how that a long time ago, back in 1900s, the D.C. Government leased land from the state of Virginia to house its inmates at the Lorton Complex. The lease contract came about because the D.C. government did not have the landscape to house their own inmates in the district. So, they drew up a lease agreement with the state of Virginia. The lease facilitated the purchase of the land for $1.00 per 1700-1800 square miles/ acres of land for one hundred years. And after the terms of the lease agreement, the land would be turned back over to the state of Virginia. Although, the actual number of acres purchased by the lease agreement have often been disputed because the seven to ten facilities actually makes up approximately 3000+ acres of Virginia state property instead of 1700+, however, the amount for the purchase has remained the same ($1.00). It is significant to note that our group discussions at work were impromptu on all accounts. But they were always shutdown by an abrupt interferences, concocted decoys, and/or emergency meetings which would end our sessions and/or discussions. With another-to-be continued part II of Lorton folklore. In closing, the gist of the matter which caused so much consternation among staff was the fact that the lease agreement for the Lorton property would be over in 2001, and from there, the Lorton prison would be closed and we would be out of our jobs and/or careers as well. But that was almost always how the rumors went. Consequently, these short rap sessions were never scheduled, just sporadic and ambivalent, perhaps to say the least, due to the nature of the casual conversations. Yet, they certainly would put a damper to any high note of the day. As previously mentioned (after abrupt endings), the sessions were shut down and we would wisp off quietly, no doubt feeling disenchanted about our career choices, while scrambling back off to our cubicles to take charge of all of our duties assigned for that day. Some of my duties and responsibilities as a case manager at the Lorton facility were as follows: ensuring the compliance of all departmental regulations and guidelines with respect to case management services. Regularly monitor department procedures relative to specific areas of classification. In addition, I would manage the supervision of approximately 100-125 inmates on my caseload, which demanded the responsibility of treatment and evaluation of each individual offender. I conducted on-site visits to the housing units to address issues that dealt with request for legal calls, provided guidance on issues related to institutional services, made referrals to mental health and psychological services, assisted in the process to expedite parole hearings, scheduled interviews that dealt with family matters and personal concerns, conducted the intake interview process, routine classifications, subsequent parole hearings, etc. With regard to classification, I conducted the classification process at least twice weekly (specifically on Wednesdays and Fridays). Now, given the awesome task of being in charge of the lives of human beings classified as wards of the state is no easy task. Theses are individuals that are separate and unique within there own rights. Each person has their own set of issues that are specific to their cases alone, so, as case managers, we have to be well organized at least to some degree. Nevertheless, the management of a caseload requires mastering the ultimate goal of time management, yet, from time to time there will be some mistakes made along the way. With that being said, after years of trials and errors and episodes that ebb and flow, one would probably be elated to find that perhaps there is a method to what often seems like sheer madness.

Some of the procedures that have been put in place have been an asset to case management services to say the least. These priorities are listed as follows:

1. Handle emergency items that affect the health, safety, or welfare of each individual inmate. This also includes death notices and seriously ill family members.
2. Review the daily movement profile for your caseload.
3. Classification for out-of-compliance cases requiring progress reports.
4. Initial parole hearings schedule for classification.
5. Parole Notice of Actions (PNOA), due within one working day of receipt.
6. Parole rehearings schedule for classification.
7. Intakes need classification (within three working days of arrival).
8. Work release/halfway house reports schedule for classification.
9. Classification for assignment to detail/removal from detail.
10. Transfer to minimum security classifications
11. Annual reviews for inmate(s) serving life terms.
12. Routine case management services/open house.

In addition, I prepared progress reports which were used by the parole board, senior department officials, the courts, and outside agencies to assist in determining the inmates' suitability for release, participating in community services programs, reduction in minimum sentence or executive clemency. Now, being a case manager was one of the most important positions that one could have. I felt blessed that god thought enough of me to put me in charge of so many individuals that needed to be processed through our criminal justice system. As a case manager, I am also required to regularly review data pertaining to the inmate's custody status under my supervision, while screening the contents on file to detect special handling requirements, escape history, mental health status, and separation orders. For the record, I perform various other assignments as well. I attend workshops, seminars, staff meeting, implement rehabilitative programs, conduct counseling sessions, supervise public relation activities, and serve on various other institutional and departmental committees, such as family day, work performance/ detail assignment committees, women's program advisory committee, etc. In addition, I regulated the operations of the intake/orientation unit, serves as chairperson for such committees serve as a member of the adjustment/ housing board, recreational, program activity committees, serves on promotion panels, community volunteer committees, etc. Furthermore, I took the initiative to implement the case management prerelease program initiative at the Occoquan facility in July 1996. The formation of this program initiative was fostered out of the utmost concern that a large segment of the inmate population lacked preparation for community transition. This program was designed to educate and inform the inmate population about the standards and expectations that would accompany the conditions of parole. Also, the program provided the inmate population with viable community resources, volunteer programs and/or professional nonprofit organizations that played a major role in the formation of successful reintegration. For the most part, this position enhanced my knowledge of the criminal justice system and its role as a partner within the scope of our communities, whereas this viable entity sought to enrich our lives and fosters safer communities. The prerelease program unleashed a renewed sense of pride, integrity and respect for which these standards are held high with professional acumen by case management services through the Lorton Complex. It is and always will be my true hope that all of our clients succeed in their recovery in all walks of life. So our role is of vital importance in their lives. As a case manager, it's very important to know how to suspense your caseload, organize your files, and monitor your daily operations so that your classifications are current, up-to-date and remain in compliance. So, one can fairly precisely determine when to schedule a case for classification. That way you could manage your caseload consistent with that suspense file and remain in compliance. For the most part, there does not exist a genuinely bonafide full-proof method for suspension of your caseload. However, there is one method that would help keep you current enough to reasonably manage the clientele on your caseload. This particular method, if implemented properly, has proven over time to be a great asset toward managing the challenges faced by staff that are professionals, who are responsible for the delivery of case management services.

Technically, the method behind the suspension process is listed as follows:

Suspension methodology:

1. You will need a small, spiral 3×4 note pad and a pen
2. First open the pad and flip to the first page
3. Next find first line at the top page, from there, find the center
4. Take the pen and write down the first month & the year (i.e., January 2012).
5. Then, flip over to the next page
6. Repeat step 3, but use the second month & the year (i.e., February 2012).
7. Keep flipping the pages until you have completed a consecutive two-to-five-year calendar.

First, after making that note pad, you will need to suspend your entire caseload. So in order to suspense your caseload, you will need all critical dates assigned to every inmate on your caseload. These dates includes: parole dates, rehears, early parole date, cadre, PNOA (Parole Notice of Actions), minimum security eligibility, halfway house eligibility, initial intakes, out-of-compliance cases, work detail assignments, custody/annual reviews, emergencies, etc. Next, clearly understand that it's not unusual for one inmate's name to appear more than once inside the note pad after being suspended to meet benchmark critical dates. For example: the parole date will be assigned to at least three different benchmarks. So first: find the parole date (i.e., critical date) and inmate's name. Second: suspend the date . . . in order to suspend, you must start by counting three months or ninety days backward from the parole date (i.e., critical date) . . . this will require that you take your notepad, flip through the pages in the note pad until you locate the date, that is three months or ninety days prior to the parole date (i.e., critical date). **Third:** find space below that top line—center page—then, on that line, write his name in the note pad for classification during that specific month for parole. Ex: if parole date is 12/4/13, than his classification for parole will be scheduled in 9/13. His halfway house classification will be in 6/13 and his minimum security transfer will be scheduled in 12/11.

Note: Parole (counts back ninety days from critical date), halfway house (counts back 180 days from critical date), and minimum security (counts back twenty-four months from critical date). As previously mentioned, these critical dates can include: early parole, parole rehears, EPA (Emergency Powers Act), cadre, work details, etc.

It is significant to note that, there was always a possibility that you could be audited. Normally, supervisor randomly audit every ninety days. So, it's a good idea to make sure to regularly review your progress reports in order to avoid out-of-compliance statuses. Upon the completion of an audit, if any progress reports were found to be in an out-of-compliance status while assigned to your caseload, you would be given a written warning, or a letter of ammunition. This letter of ammunition is then placed into your personnel file. And, if by chance, you acquired three of these letters of ammunition in your personnel file, you could be brought up on charges and subsequently suspended, dismissed and/ or fired from your job. I just truly thank God that I never received one of those, but I do know someone who did. That's exactly why, you have to be vigilant in monitoring the movement on your caseload.

From there, you can stay two steps ahead of inmate traffic without getting behind. By the way, our classification system was not automated with state of the art computer software and every crucial facet of our operation was done by hand. We did not have a personal computer. We did not have funds appropriated for the upgrading of our old antiquated computer system at work. Also, with the district being financially scrapped, for the most part, due to misallocated funds being a contributing factor to the budget crisis for that year, the new computers were off the table. Again, it's crucial to be genuinely sincere about reviewing case files daily, so that out-of-compliance statuses were neutral at ground zero (i.e., meaning that out-of-compliances cases does not exist). However, if an out-of-compliance case had been found to exist, it must be reported immediately and scheduled for classification within twenty-four hours. Therefore, the case management services team were genuinely attentive and alert. The team itself was made up a highly motivated well-established professional staff that operated under DOC policies.

One such policy for case management services was service order 4240.6. This mandate governed the guidelines for case management services at the institutional level. Hence, it oversees the requirements for the program classifications.

In facilitating the classification process, the team was required to canvass the scope of specific areas of diagnosis and treatment of each offender needs. This assessment was then incorporated with the facility's treatment program services. In addition, the mandate required that classifications be convened in the presence of a classification committee. This committee should be made up of the supervisory classification and parole officer or chief classification and parole officer, psychologist, academic teachers, vocational teachers and/or counselors, lead correctional officer, chaplain, and where applicable industrial and/or agricultural representative. Also, the final disposition of the committee members will be left up to the chief classification and parole officer. It is significant to note that the final disposition of the classification committee's recommendations will be the final authority for the offender's recommended treatment plan. And lastly, this piece of legislation stated that all cases were to be classified ninety days in advance of parole eligibility date (PED) And that the progress reports with accompanying documents would be submitted to the D.C. Board of parole at least sixty days prior to the parole eligibility date (PED).

Also, in cases where sentencing dates preclude the previous, such as EPA (Emergency Powers Act) cases, the inmate shall be classified within five days of sentencing and the progress report packet would be submitted to parole board no more than seven days later.

Furthermore, progress reports emanating from circumstances described in the aforementioned cases would contain a detailed explanation in the report's introduction section. For the record, the explanation would explain why the report had encountered any such delays.

Another purpose for this mandate was to ensure compliance with stipulation of the parties to reduce the population at the District of Columbia Detention Facility (D.C. Jail) in Campbell vs. McGruder (1985).

In 1985, the court case ruled in Campbell vs. McGruder that the D.C. Jail would not be permitted to house inmates in excess of a court ordered cap established by the D.C. Circuit court judge the oversees the population cap. And if found to be in violation, immediate charges of contempt of court would follow along with jail time days and court fees (unless otherwise specified by the courts).

Lastly, department order 4360.1 was outlined for the purposes of supplementing the court order stipulations in Campbell v. McGruder (1985). This mandate was primarily established to ensure compliance with the offender's right to receive a parole determination ten days prior to their parole eligibility date so that anyone who has met the criteria for parole maybe paroled at the earliest opportunity. Essentially, this order established the implementation of two sets of card files which contains two 3x5 file cards for each inmate incarcerated at the facility. One set was to be turned over the D.C. parole board and the other set will be kept at the facility.

The cards will contain the following information:

1. Inmate's parole eligibility date
2. Inmate's name and DCDC number
3. Name of the facility where he's confined
4. Date when he arrived
5. Police department identification number (PDID)/commitment date
6. Inmate's date of birth
7. Inmate's short-term date
8. Inmate's full-term date
9. Expedite immediately, compliance mandatory, per doc, Department of Corrections.

On any given day of the week, (albeit M-F) it was nothing for our staff to be inundated with nonstop movements from transfers and intakes. These transfers and/or intakes often included but were not limited to administrative segregation moves, emergency transfers, disciplinary transfers, protective custody request, classifications, custody review hearings, parole/halfway house transfers, etc. In fact, the case managers at the Occoquan facility in it's totality averaged approximately twelve to fifteen staff members. I was the case manager assigned to dormitories 3 and 4 at the Occoquan facility. The average individual given any knowledge of case management services would immediately understand that these numbers (as previous mentioned 100-125) were extremely too high to adequately service the inmate's population. The Occoquan facility was made up of three zones. I worked at Occoquan zone one. Once again, we managed extremely high caseload turnovers. Reportedly, the Occoquan facility has housed approximately 1,745+ inmates prompting officials to go into full frenzy mode. These were post-disturbance riot days. And the prison officials at the Lorton had been repeatedly warned that lawsuits would force them into compliance with doc policy or else face termination. Nevertheless, the pending closure of the Lorton Complex fueled the defiant flames of contempt from most staff. And they behaved accordingly. The reasons behind the increase in the Lorton population were not just one factor, there were many elements that contributed to the overcrowding. Remember, for years that the D.C. Department of Corrections (DOC) functioned as a municipal system serving in a "duel" statelike capacity for both local and state systems. So, on a local level DOC took charge of all your detained pretrials, presentence, court order warrants, probation, parole violators, short term sentence misdemeanors and felony offenders. Lastly, in addition to the aforementioned, on a state level, DOC housed all the convicted felons in the district. Nevertheless, this extremely high volume of intakes came about on the heels of increased hiring on the police force which resulted in spikes of police arrest that often included the following: (i.e., new tactics and operations to community policing), operation clean sweeps, operation bait, and switch scams along with operations like take the cake. These were all legitimate contributors. However, some of the other primary contributors included the halfway house (HWH) escape returnees, HWH tech violators, the tightening criteria for parole, the execution of mandatory minimum sentencing laws or three strikes laws (1980-1990s), drug arrest, pretrial detainees, parole violators, outstanding warrants executed, court ordered detainees, etc., all of these factors contributed to Lorton overcrowding as well. It is significant to note that a recipe for potential disaster had always plagued the Lorton population because of the combination of critical staff shortages and prison overcrowding. The prison itself routinely operated below staff compliment. Yet, without prognosticators to fore warn the future climate, many officials within the D.C. Department of Corrections were caught off guard, and became overwhelmed due to the prison overcrowding. The prison was familiar with large amounts of intakes coming in, but this most recent particular wave or massive surge came out of nowhere in late 1995. And they were taken aback on their heels and unable to regain their bearings. From there, the Occoquan facility's housing statuses were no longer considered for custody/security classifications, but, it was solely population driven. The primary basic operations of the prison system itself had to be abandoned due to overcrowding. This was a real life cruel experimental hoax that had been perpetrated on the safety and welfare of the staff and inmate population as well. The outcome of the results of this test had proven to be just as insidious as one could imagine. The overcrowding was detrimental to our population. At some point, we were literally warehousing the Lorton inmate population. Generally speaking, when there is an arrest made in the district that individual is processed at the D.C. Jail. However, the problem was that the D.C. Jail had in place a court ordered mandate (Campbell v. McGruder, 1985), which governed their population criteria, whereby the D.C. Jail could not exceed a certain number of inmates on any given day due to overcrowding. And if violations were found to have occurred, than prison officials themselves would be taken to jail and face charges of contempt of court. Now, the Lorton Complex had no such court ordered cap or population criteria, so inmates where routinely shipped down to Lorton to relieve the overflow from the jail. There have been many occasions, whereby the D.C. Jail could not clear their count due to overcrowding. Nevertheless, whenever challenged by these parameters > numerous inmates had to be loaded on buses parked in the D.C. Jail's Sallyport, (just for holdover purposes) in order to clear the count. And once the count was cleared, the jail would remove the inmates from the buses, and return to operations as usual. Our population was 95% Afro-American. However, we would still manage to get from time to time a few Caucasians, Latinos, Indian/Asian, etc. It is noteworthy that all of our inmates were treated the same regardless of race, creed, or color upon their arrival at the Occoquan facility. If one is legally deemed a convicted felon in D.C. Superior courts, then the district would be responsible for their general welfare, housing, and custody until the federal courts deem otherwise. As a result of operations at the prison being driven by the massive overcrowding throughout the Lorton facilities, the gang violence sharply increased. We noticed that more incidents of assaults, robberies, thefts, drug usage, etc., were on the rise. There were numerous incidents, whereby brutal assaults resulted in vicious attacks that escalated to cold-blooded murders. Now, these incidents were particularly unnerving given the fact that these young men lost their lives for little or nothing. In the mist of all this turmoil, the mayor, city council, police chief, etc., knew that new tactics had to be put in place to gain back control of the prison system. Also, new measures were being established for reducing overcrowding and to take on the criminal element from within.

The rallying cries of the city began to finally drum up bold support. They began a new hiring recruitment program. It was that crucial, systemic, and antiquated element within the Department of Corrections that beats back the trends of the new tidal wave in order to maintain the genre of the old. The tensions between the two entities had always existed. In fact, power has never been relinquished and given up willingly, but one has to take hold and seize it in order to bring about change. The old guard of the status quo in the department had to be dealt with, in order for the doors of opportunity to open for the new. So, new officers were hired to combat critical staff shortages. For the most part, the staff shortages were due to retirement, attrition, suspensions, transfers, turnovers, firings, etc. In addition to changes that modified staffing, the mayor also implemented and signed into law the federally mandated order to invoke the Emergency Powers Act (EPA). This order alone had a tremendous effect on the overall operations within the department. The primary goal behind this order was to relieve overcrowding. The order essentially takes the inmate's parole eligibility date (PED) from the original statutory computation and advances it by ninety days. From there, a newly established parole eligibility date (PED) will be recomputed and reflected on a new face sheet with the (EPA) sentence computations. Now, given this new facesheet reflecting the new (EPA) sentence computations, which, in most cases, would render the case out-of-compliance, immediate classification would occur. However, there were some cases in which the projected parole eligibility is so far away, until the ninety days of EPA would not make classification relevant at all. In cases like these, you just make a notation in your suspense file and keep on to the next case. As previously stated, cases with a newly established parole eligibility date (PED) as a result of (EPA) sentence computations, would be a typical textbook case for which we define in case management services as an out-of-compliance case. This means for case management services, a living nightmare because it could back log our cases for weeks and weeks at a time. This remains an arduous task for case management services to try to classify all the (EPA) mandated cases which takes priority over other assigned duties. Since these are court-ordered mandated cases, processing cannot be denied. So the agency had to pay staff overtime in order to stay within court order guidelines. There was also another method that was embraced by the agency to help relieve overcrowding. This particular method was to set up federal contracts to outsource the housing of the district's inmates in out of state contract facilities. The contracts were specifically for short-term housing purposes until the overcrowding problem could be contained. Again, case management services were hit by the agency to classify numerous groups of inmates that met the eligibility criteria for out of state transfers. Most of the out-of-state contracts were in places like Youngstown, Ohio, Waverly, VA, Sussex, VA, Pennsylvania, and Atlanta. In hindsight, this gave us an opportunity to sweep out our most vexing, diabolical, highly criminally charged inmates that qualified for removal from the Lorton Complex. So, case management staff had to work overtime on cases that met transfer criteria. These cases were then brought before a classification committee, whereby it was determined that administrative transfers were warranted due to overcrowding. I knew in the back of my mind that eventually, I would have to look for another job before the closure of Lorton or I just couldn't survive in the metro area with everything being so expensive. There was also that element of being apprehensive or ill at ease in such a dangerous work environment because our lives were at risk too. There is simply no way one can know the future, we can only make the best choices when confronted by a given set of circumstances. Yet for now, I had to deal with my reality and contend with the circumstances at hand. Nevertheless, for Lorton, the critical years of the mid-1990's were filled with ebbs and flows within the prison system. And, these seasonal changes were reflected in the highs and lows that aligned our job status as well. During the winter seasons, upon showers of ice cold drizzle that plummeted layers of freezing sleet, cascading pockets of snow and rain all over the hills side of our Temple hill, Maryland home made me nostalgic for the warmth my childhood home before the fire. As I watched outside our window with grave trepidation because I knew early morning meant that I and my little one had to venture out upon uncharted frontiers. And yet, what awaited us would be cold blankets of crystal fine porcelain pillars of snow. It is noteworthy that as winters turned to spring and summers turned to fall, there remained etched in the back of my mind which appendage chartered the order of the day. The cascades of rumors and chatter clouded the mist of our workplace. The inmates carried the tightest rumor mill operation known to tech savvy engineers. For the most part, Ms. Kelly had had her suspicions early in 1995, when inmates were found with over 10 grand in cash money and sent briefly to Maximum Security, yet promptly returned to the Occoquan Facility. Now, Ms. Kelly was somehow just too apprehensive about the turnaround of such a horrific event that got caught in the cross hairs and brought about their return without an investigation. Then, by 1997, it finally became evident to this case manager that the prison system was being hijacked by the criminal cronies/the mayor/the police department/prison officials/etc., this de jure, de facto, gestapo renegade covert government operation took advantage of a fragile, broken fleeced, discarded institution and used the prison for profit due to what was chumped—up to be its imminent demise. The mentality was just take all you can before the feds shuts everything down, that type of mindset (i.e., the D.C. National Capital Revitalization and Self-government Improvement Act of 1997 by President Clinton mandated the closure of the Lorton facilities by 2001) brought about a completely separate agenda on behalf of individuals within the agency. They all saw an opportunity to line their pockets with quick cash at the expense of public safety. So the routine protocol for the D.C. Department of Corrections was adjunct and became irrelevant. Another case in point that highlights the fleecing of the D.C. Prison system could not be more pronounced than a newspaper article leading with references being made to Robber Cave's Realistic Conflict Theory (RCT) of human behavior. The theories of Robber Cave were experiments carried out during the 1960s as duly noted in social psychology experiments researched by Robber Cave and conducted by Muzater Sherif were studies that contributed important work that researched theories about real life behaviors in controlled environments. In Cave's day, officers, and religious volunteers didn't moonlight in crime, either-or if they did, they didn't get caught, unlike the twenty-three corrections officers police arrested in 1993 for smuggling drugs to inmates for money, or the 38 individuals posing as Muslim religious volunteers police charged in 1996 with sneaking drugs and prostitutes into Lorton. That same year, maximum-security inmate Keith Gaffney was convicted of running a heroin-distribution ring from his cell that employed not only other inmates but corrections officers as well. This article printed from "The Washington city paper," by Annys Shin, March 9, 2001. Now it is significant to note that for years, the District of Columbia had been warned to build more prisons down at the Lorton Complex due to a projected crime surge in the streets of D.C. The city mayor had attended numerous city council meetings where by the police, city commissioners, school boards, union members, lawyers, contractors, vendors, etc., all were informed of the critical need to build more prisons for an ever exploding crime rate that was on the verge about to paralyze the D.C. Metro Area. This was in the mist of the city literally going broke due to a deficit in excess of three million dollars in 1995. This has been a perpetual fight between the mayor and the financial control board to keep pace with the city's crime wave which prompted the hiring and training of police, building prisons, city repairs of schools, payroll, water, power and electric, bridges, highways, etc. In order to get a clear understanding about the tension for years between the mayor and the congress over the district's affairs, you would have to revisit homerule. Homerule for the district was achieved in 1973 through legislative measures that permitted the district limited powers over its own affairs. In fact, congress retained oversight over the city's budget and laws in spite of being granted homerule. The district would continue a strained relationship with the congress for many years to come. But in 1990, D.C. appeared to be gaining ground when it was granted surrogate powers over its owns affairs. Well, this too many amounted to positive strides toward statehood. In fact, this status had never been achieved before. Then, with this new found status congress permitted the district to symbolically appoint a member in the senate and the house to represent the District in Congress. Yet, these members had no power, no pay, and no vote. The D.C. community has contempt for it's present condition regarding homerule. And, this was primarily due to some legitimate well documented concerns that the D.C. Community is being denied full representation by congressional voting rights, yet their citizens pay amongst the highest taxes in the land. To date, the residents of the district continue to fight for their rights with the contention that taxation without representation amounts to an egregious violation of their constitutional rights. Furthermore, it is dictated by the constitution that every citizen of this United States be endowed by the 14th amendment which makes it null and void for legislation to promote the notion of taxation without representation. See www.dcvote. org. In 1868, the 14th amendment to the U.S. Constitution was ratified and states that "No state shall make or enforce law which shall abridge the privileges or immunities of citizens of the United States; nor shall any state deprive any person of life, liberty, or property without due process of law; nor deny to any person within its jurisdiction the equal protection of the laws." The real reasoning behind the district's financial crisis was not solely due to mismanagement of funds. There were other mitigating factors that contributed to their financial ruin. In the first place, the congress forbidden the district to tax federal properties in and around the district that it has declared public domain, yet, required the district to sponsor the upkeep, maintenance, and operations of such properties (i.e., museums, monuments, historical sites, and/or reservations, etc). Keep in mind that congress never fully appropriated the funds to accommodate these services. In addition, there were concerns that involved the federal retirement system for employees of the district that are entitled to federal pensions, yet, congress has failed to backup their pension plans as required by law, leaving the district to shoulder this burden on its own. Also, the district experienced suburban flight due to Washington, D.C. Being dubbed back in the early 1990s as "the murder capital of the world." In addition, Mayor Marion Barry was arrested January 18, 1990 and subsequently convicted for possession of crack cocaine in the

1990s. Not only was this a sad day for the citizens of the District of Columbia but for the mayor as well. So, here you have a capital city decimated by urban flight, overwhelmed by creditors saber rattling their coffers drowning in debt, on the verge of bankruptcy, and abandoned by the United States congressional bank roll this haphazard multifaceted crisis in Washington, D.C. Left little hope for the District of Columbia's dream to overcome what is perceived by many of its citizens as federal oppression. The laws passed by congress that approves the district's purse string leaves it decimated within the scope of financially ruin. At some point, the district was put under receivership due to its lack of fiscal responsibility. Hence, the district's financial affairs were then controlled by several entities such as the mayor, the congress, the D.C. City council, and the financial control board. During much of the 1990s, the day to day operations of the city itself was extremely limited on cash flow. As previously mentioned, the city lost a sizable portion of its tax base due to residents opting to relocate to neighboring counties in Maryland and Virginia primarily due to high crime. Since, the early '90s, the city has been scrapped to keep pace with the crime wave that hit from crack cocaine. This crack cocaine epidemic has simply mortified the whole Washington D.C. Area. In fact, this massive flood of illegal narcotics prompted police to aggressively pursue criminal activity involving illegal drugs. So, the police chief, Chief Ramsey, initiated an operation clean sweep public safety program. These programs did stem the tidal wave of drug crimes, yet they drove a massive career savvy, street smart, and highly sophisticated inmate into the district's overwhelmed prison system. In fact, two new prisons were built within the last year, (1994-1995, respectively) just prior to the court's mandate for Lorton closure being signed into law 1997. The modular facility and the youth center (two). Yet, this did not handle the ever increasing overcrowding problem for the District of Columbia because the politicians waited too late to cease the opportunity to head off this crisis. In fact, both of the prisons were at their capacity within months after being opened. Therefore, our work at the prison became a war zone. You see, to live and work inside an inept prison environment is synonymous with being trapped in the belly of the beast. Once this operation was set into motion at the top, it was no turning it around. It could not be shut off. Too many heads would roll. The ax would fall too deep. There was no other option except to allow this beast/concoction to play itself out. As previously stated, the overcrowding at some point became alarming. In fact, it was the overcrowding, on many levels that was responsible for the senseless violence. Then too many individuals formulated this insane notion from an eerie ominous belief that crime pays among thieves. So criminals began promoting a weird concocted accusation that "I can be literally *crime-free* from inside instead of being on the outside looking in. This meaning that I can be *free* to do all the crime I want at this Lorton prison on the inside instead of on the outside looking in. "Well, with that being said, big time well-known D.C. Gang bangers, high rollers, thugs, etc., All wanted a piece of the action. They all jumped at chance to move their criminal enterprises inside the prison to set up shop. To them, it was an opportunity to bank roll a career with record profits. Many of them hoped to stack up the money and send it home to their families. Or stash it in a safe place until they were back on the streets. To them, it was a business proposition. No different than the ones they carried out on the street. They were on the verge of making more money than ever in their lifetime. Probably. The biggest in their career. This was a brilliant idea. Unfortunately. There would be casualties from war and this would be no exception. As a matter of fact, this whole operation had taken on a life of its own. It evolved into a full-fledge revolution. The lines were already drawn in the sand. There is much to be said about greed and where it takes us. It is difficult to gage when ruthless individuals behave badly. These are just some ideas that I summed up on my own. So I wrote this poem and called it no boundaries.

NO BOUNDARIES

The evil that men do causes actions with no boundaries. His hatred is as vast and wide as the deep blue sea. He creeps all night and roams all day to devour the likes of his prey hence, he devises one scheme after another to destroy each soul that maintains the struggle even though he appears on the scene without reproach, he is the sole source of all corruption, strife and pride of life. He has no boundaries.

To mankind this is a vicious diabolical plan to sift as wheat, all whom seek harmony, love and peace, in the way god created this world to be. The routine course of each single day is intricately designed to cast all hope away. How can the very evil be elevated to the very top when the struggle is ignored and simply dropped? Why is the scoundrel seemingly the apple of God's eye when one struggles so hard to go on just to be denied? How can the devil be allowed a free pass to attack at will, when mankind's struggle is exploited by an uneven playing field. Why has the world bought into deception spawn by wicked lies, when all that is evil is mocked for good and wrapped in disguise. There's just not much left to put aside, except that man and all of his evil deeds must be exposed and denied. Isa. 32:3

- After many years of coming in and out of the Lorton prison system like a revolving door, most D.C. inmates have adopted the prison system as a rites of passage, apart of their culture or legacy that's incorporated from their neighborhood. In fact, almost everyone from D.C. and/ or the surrounding area knows of someone serving time at Lorton or related (i.e., family members) to someone connected in some form or fashion to the Lorton reformatory. These young men are indoctrinated at an early age. From the start, many from birth are left alone or abandon in order to fend for themselves. In this particular situation, the government subsidized by tax payers have to step in and perpetrate the role of caretaker. Although it be solely lacking in many respects to the foundation of a traditional family setting, it's far better than not having resources available at all. Again, there lies another legacy of abandonment from which we have already seen in the prison system. So their childhood experiences were never formulated via nurture, nor assimilated to implore balance, guidance, and structure. It has very often been bruised, or emasculated. Their innocence is lost, and they grow up far too soon. They are simply a product of their own environment where by we as a society must seek to find what makes these young men whole again. They are forced to be equipped to handle maturity at an adulthood status with little or inadequate experience. Unfortunately, in most cases, there was no experience at all. Yet, and still, within the mix there lies in and of itself the game changer. At some point, it is not a matter of if, but when will this individual cross the line that may or may not cost his life or his freedom. From there, the prison culture is inebriated with young Afro-American males who are misguided, lacks discipline, uneducated, morally and/or financially bankrupt, etc. they are ill-equipped to deal with the realities of a criminal lifestyle. The thug life culture has been apart of the prison system all along. In fact, they are in and of itself one in the same. In looking at the genesis of this moral decay, one can start with the home. Most young Afro-American men born in Washington, D.C. arrive on the scene being dubbed by two familiar terms which defines them for the better part of their lives. Most of our Afro-American men derive from what is often defined as low-income, and single female headed households. Now, there are an array of factors that might have led to women raising a child in a nontraditional family status or single-parent household. But that still does not always mean she can't beat the odds. For the most part, the source of a myriad of deep seated, systemic, adverse conditions throughout the black community is centered around poverty. Nevertheless, the average black woman grew-up wanting to be married and wanting to have a white-picketed fenced with two and a half kids. This whole scenario plays itself out through different stages of our lives, time and time again, hoping to raise a strong healthy family with the desire to watch them grow-up to be successful young men and women. So black people desire the same successes for their families as any other red-blooded American citizen would like for their households, but, for the black community, in cases more often than not, our dreams have to be abandoned, deferred or denied. From there, for the black community's plan-b (i.e., keep marching on) has to kick in. We are a loving, hard working community for the most part, who generally don't believe in abortions, so we reach out to every resource available to fight for the survival of that child. We as black women, if given the situation of being left alone with a fatherless child, we will continue on and raise that child. So let the record reflect that the black community is not looking for a hand-out, but a helping hand. We, as black women, will raise that child and never look back. For it is a known fact that the black community has weathered almost every kind of storm known to man. So being fatherless in the black community is just another cross to bear. We have been taught how to find a way to stand strong. With that being said, we know how to look to the hills, from whence comes our strength, for our strength cometh from the lord (Ps. 121:1). So deep inside the soul, we will find the strength and the dignity to carry on. But despite the circumstances, we will continue on, always head held high, always moving forward. Consequently, this is a heavy cross to bear because it destroys black unity and promotes poverty, whereas, both are bitter pills to swallow. Yet, for almost every generation in the black community, this has been done, just as during the times of slavery. As discoveries were made throughout the past, it became evident that the first slave ship (Dutch ship traced back to the year 1619) that docked the shores of North America (Jamestown, Virginia) in the 16th century were poised to ravage the spoils of their ill found gains. The records will reflect that the ultimate price paid for the purchase of slave labor was the down fall of the Afro-American race. Our people were stolen from their homeland in Africa. They were loaded aboard ships as human cargo, and packed like sardines in the belly of British ships. From there, they were forced to endure a perilous voyage across the Atlantic Ocean. This journey resulted in millions that lost their lives due to famine, sickness, and disease. This was such an egregious massacre, that this particular voyage became known as the middle passage. Even if they were able to survive the journey alive, they were beaten, stripped of all dignity and sold off as slaves into a life time of servitude. Now, here we see again, the callous disregard for the family unit. The institution of slavery created a legacy of fatherless homes throughout the black community, and the remnants of this atrocity is evident today. For example, see how the husbands were taken away from their wives. The children were often times removed from their mothers and sold separate and apart. Even though hundreds of decades have gone bye, the laws have never been laid out to bear homage, respecting the descendents of African slaves to have an opportunity for an equal playing field on American soil. The law is still laid out for the rich to play by a different set of rules than the poor. And, the fact still remains that the laws cannot legislate the hearts of man. Be that as it may, president Abraham Lincoln invoked an executive order calling for an end to slavery in America when he signed the emancipation proclamation in 1863. Nevertheless, continued rebellion throughout the states remained prevalent in order to retain slave labor. So we saw Jim Crow laws reign supreme throughout the land across the south. In 1865, after President Abraham Lincoln signed the thirteenth (13th) amendment which outlawed slavery in the United States, we continued to revisited the slave culture mentality time and time again. With that being said, the spirit of the law must be eclipsed by the letter of the law. Also, what a man thinketh in his heart, so is he. Therefore, if bigotry, pride, arrogance, greed, hatred, racism, and prejudice lie in his heart, than no law in the land can make him comply otherwise. Even if the laws could redress some of the malice and contempt and bigotry by legislating a color blind society for which freedom of life, liberty, and pursuit of happiness reign supreme in the land, then again the first step would be for each one to follow these laws. Therefore, just look at poverty in America from twenty to thirty years ago (1983-1993) whereas approximately fourteen million people reportedly were living in poverty, yet, compare that with fellow Americans living today (2012) in poverty which accounts for some (forty-six million people). Then, you can see why it still remains at epidemic proportions in America today. This is crucial because as mentioned earlier, notwithstanding the bitter pill of slavery, the main source of a myriad of deep seated systemic adverse conditions throughout the black community is centered-around poverty. In a book called *My Soul Looks Back in Wonder*, by Juan Williams, foreword by David Halberstam, and afterword by Marian Wright Edelman, pp. 213, the struggle of the plight of the black man's state of affairs is highlighted. Dr. King remained us that when our nation's founders wrote the declaration of independence and the constitution, they created a promissory note guaranteeing all Americans the inalienable rights of life, liberty and pursuit of happiness. But America had defaulted on that promise for black Americans and issued a check that had come back marked "insufficient funds."

Dr. king refused to believe "the bank of justice is bankrupt," so do I. America's promised commitment to justice must converge with our great wealth to end poverty and hopelessness for millions of people. Forty years after, Dr. King dreamed of a day when his own children would be judged "not by the color of their skin but by the content of their character," it is intolerable that the gap between rich and poor is widening, and that huge disparities of opportunities persist for black children.

1. In 1988, 11 million children were poor. In 2002, twelve million children were poor.
2. Three out of ten black children are poor. Black children are more than twice as likely as white children to live in poverty.
3. Overall infant mortality rates have declined, but they have declined faster for white children than for black. Black babies are about two-and-?-half times more likely to die than white babies in the first year.
4. Black women are about three times likelier than white women to die as a result of complications from pregnancy or childbirth.
5. High school dropout rates have declined for black and white students, but black students remain almost twice as likely as whites to drop out—the same ratio as in 1963.
6. If current trends continue, black males will be five times more likely than white males to be incarcerated. Almost one in every three black males will have spent some time in prison during his life.

Theoretically speaking, specific areas of concentration are established within the ranks of a professional organization. In fact, such organizations thrive on the concept of employee morale, professional work ethics, program ingenuity, managerial training, etc., which are all considered standard operational procedure within the scope of departmental policy. Most of these concepts are crucial to explore and vital to the overall function of the organization. Given the routine operations of a correctional institution (i.e., prison), certain concepts should be employed. For example, these can often include the following, but, are not limited to: academic/vocational training programs, religious faith base services, library services, mental health services, social/recreational programs, health care services, etc. It is also incumbent upon the institution to establish policies and procedures which provide the inmate population with a catalyst by which they can challenge the discretion of departmental policies. From there, implement a classification team, headed up by a comprehensive diagnostic team which in turn formulates the housing requirements and the stabilization of the operation as a whole. These are among the essential fundamentals of basic operations. Now, when these components were established as the foundation, yet, subsequently were eroded by one's personal agenda separate and apart from the principles cited above. Then we no longer have a program that can be sustained. If our mission has failed, than the welfare and safety of our staff and inmate population alike becomes compromised. Furthermore, we carry the burden of custodial civil servants, yet, the public's safety then becomes at risk. As we closely examine the demise of our criminal justice system at the Lorton Complex, we began to see just how murky the waters transcended the currents beyond its shores . . . particularly in our prison system, we have found that on each occasion the culprit behind the compromise within our jaded system was one's personal agenda. These measures threaten the lives of all. Unfortunately, some lives were lost in the process as well. The Complexities within this Washington, D.C. Lorton prison system were exploited by a sophisticated coup of elite personnel with their own personal agenda. The power moves extended across the aisle to the inmate population, the management operations within the institutions, the union management, the halfway houses, the parole board, the city council, the mayor, the police, etc. Reportedly, the records will undoubtly reflect what will begin to surface is that many facets of power plays emerged whereby each agent exploits its own agenda. These were crucial times for the Lorton Complex as time was whining down toward the closure of the Lorton compound. Unfortunately, concessions were made and they were adhered to by the powers to be. Again, this was primarily due to a culture of corruption in crisis spiraling out of control. And the culture itself was not really unique within the prison system. But this system was tantamount to a tidal wave of one's worst nightmares that just appeared on the scene with brutal malice and forethought. Nevertheless, be that as it may, each component that made up a management team had to by happenstance ride out the storm.

Let's take a moment to examine the women and their role in the dynamics of the prison system at Lorton. Originally, women were not even allowed to work in the prison system statewide. It took the women to pursue their rights to work in jobs that were preserved exclusively for men by filing lawsuits in federal court. Most male dominated professions like police, military, construction, transportation, etc, which were considered off limits to women until the passage of Title VII of the Civil Rights Act of 1964. The women battled both racial and sexual integration cases in the federal courts despite the seemingly slow progress that their efforts made. Reportedly, the D.C. Department of Corrections hired the first class of women to work in the D.C. prison system at Lorton in the mid 1970s. And that course of action prompted women to set in motion a fire storm of lawsuits in the federal courts for being denied their civil rights in the workplace. Many of the battles were some of which were being fought throughout the transition process that finalized the forum for the Lorton closure. So the D.C Department of Corrections women had to fight many battles on many frontiers. Although women were the minority in the work force they were treated like second class citizens when compared to their male counter parts. The behavior of sexual explicit acts both verbally and/or physically were so outrageous until lawsuits among the female frontline staff and management staff as well began to surface rapidly from the late 1980s through the early 1990s. Of course this entire process required ongoing investigations that stymied the final dispositions and solely hamstrung much of the judicial process. At some point, female staff quickly began to realize that many co-workers or their colleagues circumvented the lawsuit process because it stayed in litigation so long without seemingly staunch redress. Reportedly, it stayed before the court for very long periods of time and cost extremely large amount of money, not to mention the vast number hours lost in wages from work. They realized how easy it was to get promotions in the Department of Corrections when all they had to do was sleep with some high-minded elite, hot shot, shady character with a fancy title and stand back and watch their careers take flight and their salaries rise. Needless to say that some bed feathers were searching for more than a one night stand or a booty call. Some of the chicken head females thought they were in love. In certain cases, when both parties involved were two consenting adults, the added incentive of subsequent promotions just made the whole deal impossible to past up. Nevertheless, after the sexual favors or quid pro quo, the participants had a new title, consecutive promotions, and bragging rights. At that point, women began leading the pack with their own agenda in efforts to garner position and power to play in the big leagues. And for them, the bottom line from the start was to achieve the position or title that they had rightfully earned through their own hard work. So, to get their promotions by any means necessary was somewhat bittersweet for some. From there, internal conflict began. Some staff members refused to stoop that low and compromise their integrity for something that was rightfully theirs in the first place. So, groups were divided on the issue and stood their ground. They hired attorneys, set up shop prepping their cases, while standing their ground and vowing to fight back for the long haul. The women that stood their ground knew that they were in for the fight of their life. And that was only the beginning. They were victims of retaliation as well. In hindsight, one lawsuit would just lead to another. Needless to say, that amounted to more court battles within the D.C. Department of Corrections. Yet many women felt that it was worth the fight in the end. With the publicity from lawsuits for sexual harassment so rampant in the mid 1990s, the mayor **Mr. Juan Freeman** came forth in a formal meeting with departmental heads to announce the launch of a new departmental policy for sexual harassment in the workplace. In addition, he aimed **to quale** some of the high sprung rhetoric citing defamation of character through dirty leaks. Essentially, he wanted to tamper some of the rancor and calm contempt among department employees. By 1995, this campaign for the new policy became department wide and promoted zero tolerance for sexual harassment in the workplace. Initially, the message was not well received from the mayor. It was taken by many as a joke due to his less than stellar drug past (in 1990 arrested for crack cocaine) and the rumors of his extramarital affairs. Nevertheless, the order was sanctioned by the federal courts to be mandated as the law that was ordered to rule the infamous DOC agency. Then, rumors began to surface that spreads a diatribe of scandalous verbal assaults among management staff department-wide. From there, classified information surfaced about the content of the specifics of certain lawsuits. Sometimes, the rumors were about who got subpoenas or who did not and what was allegedly said. Also, some information leaked out about the content exchanged during the depositions in certain high-profile cases. These items were crucial to both the trial judges and attorneys as well. Not to mention the potential damage to the plaintiff's case being tried in court. Nevertheless, these leaks created a dangerously hostile workplace environment. And it seemed to be someone who knew a lot about departmental gossip. Because every time the information was released, DOC went into panic mode. They tried to launch a full-scale investigation to root out the parties involved. And 500 C street, Vermont Ave., Washington, D.C. 20023, blew its top. But the culprits have never been caught. To date, no one knew how the idea got started. But whenever there was high-profile breaking news or vicious rumors involving high-profile staff members, the culprits would tell all details in an anonymous, 8x10 double spaced, two-to-three-paged typed letter. Their mode of dissemination was to pass out letters hand-to-hand or use departmental mail carriers via shotgun envelopes. The people behind this overall operation were well-trained, highly skilled, protocol elite, and sophisticated individuals. They had to know people in high places as well. Initially, the *operation appeared to start out as an experimental prank or roust.* I remember seeing the first one found in our unit. It was found by one of our case managers in the mail box. She said she read it, and then she made about twenty something copies and handed them out to everybody she knew. So it just simply caught on like wild fire. Whenever a copy came out, they just flew all over the Lorton Complex like hotcakes. It was a known fact that everybody, everywhere had to have one. Staff would just wait on baited breathe to get the next one just to find out who was doing what? And what was gonna be the next shoe to drop? These were the hottest gossip tips of the day. They had no schedule or timeframes and appeared randomly unannounced. And unfortunately most of all of them were 90-95% true. The party or parties involved in the creation of these letters called them "**DID YOU KNOW?**" Quite frankly, there was no introduction to the letters. In fact, after the caption title at the top, the letters begin (from paragraph one) by jumping right into the latest gossip. While reading this one particular letter keep in mind some highlights:

1. Confrontations that were allegedly inferred amongst staff were duly noted yet primarily responsible for the angst, stressed, and/or extremely tensed, and potentially hostile work environment.
2. Pay especially attention to the animosity that surfaced with regard to both aspects of racial and gender integration in the workplace.
3. Check out the tone set between management and the frontline staff with respect to being firm, fair, and consistent with matters of brutal career defining moments.

DID YOU KNOW?

Mr. Neveille Pratt (Caucasian)
Associate Director of Institutions
Mr. George Leverte (Caucasian)
Chairman, Fraternal Order of Police (FOP)
Department of Corrections Labor Committee
Ms. Palin Joyce (African-American)
Director of D.C. Department of Corrections

Did you know, that Messrs. Nev **Pratt** and George **Leverte** are running Corrections? Did you know that they both testified in court and gave their depositions in the **Steele vs. Corrections** case; regarding their improper sexual relationship with a female who works on **Leverte's** staff?

Did you know that **Pratt** brought this female back to work with Corrections after her three years had expired? He then tried to get a certain administrator to give her a promotion after she had been back for only ninety days. How many other people did you give early promotions to that year **Pratt**?

Did you know that this same female was retained on **Leverte's** staff even after all correctional officers were supposedly being sent back to their positions? Pratt also kept his detailed correctional officer (female). Why was that allowed?

Did you know that the female in **Leverte's** shop was given a promotion (supervisory) over other more qualified individuals? Why?

Did you know that during the *Steele vs. Corrections* trials that two other females with sterling reputations, made sexual harassment allegations against **Pratt** in open court? It was also made crystal clear that Ms. Samuels made a deal with **Pratt** for subsequent promotions to withdraw her sexual harassment complaint (16 pages in all).

Did you know that our director, **Palin Joyce,** knows all of this?

Did you know that **Pratt** and **Leverte** are deeply involved in the reorganization plan for Corrections? Why?

Did you know that **Leverte** routinely uses vulgar and condescending language that is directed at his subordinates? His recent gaff in the

Washington Post is typical of the disdain that he has for Corrections workers in general. Yet, he remains in power in Corrections. Why? Our director, **Palin Joyce**, even saw fit to support **Leverte's** so-called apology letter. Why?

Does she feel it is okay for Caucasians (white males) to insult and harass/ harangue Afro-American folk with impunity? After all history has recorded, George Washington and Thomas Jefferson as taking liberties with their female slaves. Does our director consider this part of tradition? Does she think that this is just the cost of succeeding in America? Is she just all bark and no bite? It just goes to show "you can take some black folk off the plantation but you can't take the plantation out of some black folk." Shame on you, **Palin Joyce**.

Have you watched the pattern our director has established in alleged harassment cases? Persecution for Afro-American males and denial and excuses for Caucasians (white males), does that tell us something? It is the feeling of many that Ms. Joyce would not have made her now infamous trek to visit those Correction Officer Supervisor; if one of them (Joe Dirt) had not been Caucasian (white male). Think about it, how many Afro-American males has she openly shown her support for?

What has been observed from Palin Joyce's actions over the last two years is an assault on and an insult to the "basic rights" of many Corrections employees. Her conspiring with lowly white males (Pratt and Leverte) is the equivalent of a Hatfield fraternizing with a McCoy.

Did you know that **Leverte** with the knowledge/direction of Palin Joyce has conducted surreptitious criminal background checks (NCIC) on current and former corrections employees? Tell us Ms. Joyce, who's going to check **Leverte's** criminal history? **Pratt's** too?

Did you know that there were plans to covertly check criminal backgrounds for all current corrections employees? We were told that was nothing but a ruse to target all those individuals who have filed or testified in the ongoing case of *Stelle vs. Corrections*. This is unconstitutional and illegal repeal of the conditions of employment for every employee in this department. But unfortunately, it is classic Palin Joyce. **FRATERNAL ORDER OF POLICE-(FOP) OR UNION REPS (DOC) WHERE IN THE HELL ARE YOU?**

Our director has taken us further back than the oppression of women in the United States during the 1840s. She has taken us back to the Women's

Suffrage Movement where America exploits a woman's rights to have the dignity to vote just like her men counter parts in America who freely have their voices heard. This director really enjoys the concept of a showcase on display. She likes the idea of women being seen, but she will go the extra 10th degree to make sure that they are not heard. She just does not get it. It makes you wonder how she achieved her status in the majority white male dominated Pennsylvania system.

Our director gets a hardy vote of **NO CONFIDENCE** from the black females in this agency.

Sincerely, can't wait to get the hell out of Lorton!

Now this particular letter was only a sample of the many letters that routinely appeared on the scene of work stations throughout Lorton. Upon being discovered, nobody seemed to know their origin or if they had any knowledge refused to come forth. To this date, the agency has not been able to determine their source. This has caused the department lots of grief. And this has complicated many court cases pending in U.S. Superior Court. The final disposition in many of these cases has yet to be determined as they remain in litigation without resolution. Unfortunately, an alarming number of them have already been dismissed without prejudice. Ironically, this is the price that the litigants were willing to pay for the price of victory in the face of defeat. Many of the women with sexual misconduct cases continued their litigation throughout the facility closure. And there were many others that just gave up trying. But much of this culture of misogyny in the department has stemmed the tide for hopeful possibilities for equality for women in the workplace. Nevertheless, the battle for equal rights for women continues to live on.

So, Jimmy Black was very familiar with the street life. He was raised by the streets in a single-parent household without a father figure in his life. He grew up at war with much of the world. He secretly longed for a father to teach him how to be a man and resented the fact the he had to teach himself. All his life all he has ever known is war.

JIMMY EXPLORES HIGH-STAKES DRAMA

With corruption so wide spread, it was hard to determine who was really playing by the rules. In other words, how could one know for sure who was true to the game? Now being locked up in prison doing time ain't no joke.

For real, I declare, these niggars gone make me lose my mind up in here. I need access to certain operations to get my product showcased on the floor. So, let's get this straight up front on the first try. Honest to god no misunderstandings. I want some mules, a stable, and some hay, hay, hay! You know how we roll. Yeah, that's right, now, you know how we roll. Once I gained entrance up in this piece, I can roll. From there, I can get my homies to front for me, that's all I need. my street crew is good enough for me, I don't trust these niggars up in here. You got that. I want a work squad crew approved for duty first thing Monday morning. I need me at least four or maybe five cell phones, fresh as a kite. They got to be fresh ones, no tracers. As soon as you move on that, I can handle my business and get my hustle on. Hey, one last thing, don't call, harass, disturb, or complain to me about shit, 'til . . . you man up! You feel me, homie. Hollar at yoy niggar . . . duce. I'm out, peace . . . check me later.

Now, Jimmy Black was born and raised in the nation's capital. He resided in a low-income housing project, S.E. Barry farms, Washington, D.C. where he lived with his mother and four siblings. As far as family goes, his mother, Tahoe Blango, was all he had. Now, Tahoe was young when she became pregnant with jimmy. She was from a mixed culture herself. Her mom was American-Indian, French, Afro-American, and Puerto Rican. Her father was Caucasian. She was eighteen years old and a senior in high school, but she never did graduate with her senior class. When he first laid eyes on Tahoe, he had to have her. To him, it didn't matter what she cost. He just made his mind up that he wouldn't be taking no for an answer. She was originally from Louisiana, French quarters. But he was not. He had one objective in mind. He didn't care anyway, 'cause all he wanted was a piece of that fine brown ass. He was in the middle of a drug deal when he saw her on her way home from school one day. She was approached by him that same day. And in the bed spreaded eagle that same night. Tahoe was a virgin at the time. She was not aware that a pregnancy could even happen the first time. But in her case, it did. Shortly after that, as the months past bye, Tahoe continued the sex. She knew that it was wrong, but he had become so aggressive that she was afraid to say no. Then, after she had repeated the act three or four more times, she told him she was not feeling well. One day, she went to the drug store and bought a pregnancy test. After she took the test, the results came back positive. Well, the next day, Tahoe gave her mother the news, and her mother kicked her out of the house. So, Tahoe was left standing on the streets of the main thoroughfare in the heart of the French quarters. And nestled by her side was a duffle bag with what appeared to be all the belongings that she had. Then, from out of nowhere, here comes the man. He motions for

Tahoe to get inside the four-door, tinted window, **black cadillac**, stretched limo-sized SUV. Tahoe got inside the SUV, but the first five minutes, she didn't speak, she just cried. "Well, is there something that you need to say?" he asked. "I'm just stressed right now, please, I need a few more minutes." He answered eagerly, "Hey, it's okay, okay. I can do that, is that all? Right, okay, I got that. Tahoe, I got you." From there, it was a long silence before she could regain her composure. Yet, he was willing to just drive to the end of the earth, if that's how much time that she needed. After she calmed herself down, she began to explain about their child that she was carrying and about how much she wanted to keep their child. But then, she said her mother had given her an ultimatum to choose an abortion or leave. She said that when she refused to agree to have the abortion, her mother kicked her out. Tahoe felt abandon by her mom. She screamed, "Help me," and began crying all over again. She kept repeating over and over again, "Help me, help me, my whole world is falling apart." Finally, he was able to calm Tahoe down, and he got her to stop crying. He could tell that all of that stress was not good for her, or his unborn child. So at that point, he did feel that most of this was actually his fault, and by that being his child, he felt obligated to do right by Tahoe. He had thought about leaving earlier, but with this situation at hand, he just couldn't abandon her now. He just felt that that was the least that he could do. After, she was relaxed, and calmed down, she fell asleep as he cruised throughout the city streets in town. This quiet time allowed him to rethink his plans for the future. So after driving around, he finally took her to his house, and got her settled inside so she could rest much better. After that, he stepped back outside to collect his thoughts. While pacing through the backside of his freshly cut manicured lawn, he recalled his 2:00 a.m. drug deal. It was all that stood between his plans to ice the big e-z and be scott-free. He had also decided to give up the hard-core thug life, go straight and raise his kid, and finally make Tahoe his wife. The next thing he thought to himself was, I'm not getting any younger and this damn thug life is wearing me down. I really need to make some serious grown man moves. But for now, I got to go finish my business deal, and maybe, just maybe that will put a little free time on my schedule. Hopefully, that will buy me and Tahoe a mini vacation. When he looked back at the Rolex on his wrist, it was 12:40 a.m. He had just enough time to drop the move on this last deal. So he went up to his loft to get ready. As he glanced over to the petition adjacent to his bed, Tahoe was still sleeping, quietly, like a babe. So he never turned on the lights. He could literally get all that was needed together for the move on this deal with his eyes closed. Remember, this was his life for the past twelve to fourteen years, and he had built-up street rep with big named clientele on the drug market. His business was nothing but a true beast. He ran it just like a lean, mean, stealth machine. He always worked alone, and he liked to keep it that way. So at 2:00 a.m., he made the drop on his deal. The bank had hit the wire by 2:40 a.m., and just like clock work, his deal was done. So he drove straight back to the house to check on Tahoe.

Now Carleen had finally settled down in her job at the prison. She had met a young man briefly for which she had dated a couple of years. Carleen met her baby's daddy on a trip to Pentagon City Mall in Arlington, Virginia. She had won a riffle ticket at work which came with a package deal. It cost $20.00 to win a trip to the spa, a matinee and dinner for two. The deal came with no expiration date. In fact, the most attractive feature of the whole deal to Carleen was the fact that there was no expiration date. So she thought to herself, why not just buy one. And she did. But then, she won. Shortly after that, she took some time off work and went to the mall. Actually, with regard to the timeline, she took off two weeks from work and it was approaching the weekend of her second week. In fact, it was early Sunday morning that she decided to strike out on her trip to Pentagon City Mall. The weather was beautiful that day. As she walked along the main thoroughfare toward the entrance to the mall, there he quickly emerged from the busy crowd, holding open the door for her to walk through. It was instant magic between the both of them. It was as if he was waiting for her all along. And to Carleen, it was like he was all that she had been waiting for. He was tall, about 6'3", medium brown, dark skinned, well-groomed, and beautiful smile. The romance took off like a rocket to the moon. Even though the relationship did not survive their busy lifestyles, it produced a beautiful baby girl. Carleen was a wonderful mom, and she was very proud of her baby girl. Despite the stigma of being a single black female, Carleen raised her child with dignity and pride in the suburbs of Oxon Hill, Maryland. They lived in a beautiful brick two-story house. The years went by quickly and Carleen's baby girl grew fast. From the time that she was a small child, Carleen would get her up every morning by 6:00 a.m. Carleen made sure that her baby girl followed a good health regime established from her youth. She was taught at a very young age to brush her teeth, wash her face, comb her hair, shower, and bathe. Of course, as her kid got older, these chores specifically hygiene, along with household chores were less cumbersome. And now a days, most of the household chores were being shared by the two of them. This change was a big help for Carleen, all of which she welcomed very much. When you take into account that she had to get up early in the mornings, get her kid fed and ready for school. Then drive her to the daycare center, drop her off, and then head out to Lorton, Virginia to go to work, this was extraordinary. In addition, at the end of the day, she had to pick her up from daycare, make it safely home, and then, turn around tomorrow, and do the same thing again. Usually, this was a forty to fifty minute commute that she made every day, come rain, snow or shine. It is significant to note that it was an extraordinary fact to say the least that Carleen herself nor did her daughter miss very many days, despite their hectic schedules. Carleen often longed for her baby's daddy, and he would sometimes call her on holidays. In fact, her last postcard that she received from him came from Baton Rouge, Louisiana. But Carleen, never spoke a bad word about her daughter's father. She would always let it be known that her dad loved her very much.

Well, Tahoe was good and rested after that long nap. She awoke well refreshed, but very hungry. As soon as she opened her eyes, her man was seated directly across from her, perched on the edge of his chair patiently waiting. Tahoe slowly began to rub her eyes to clear up her focus, and then she said, "What time is it? Did I take too much of your time?" Then as he looked directly into her eyes, he slowly began to speak. "Look, Tahoe, I've been thinking, and I suggest that you stay here with me, for now. Then, in a couple of months or so, I suggest that we leave this place all together for good, and relocate to Washington, D.C. Tahoe at first seemed confused, but she was too weak and too hungry to argue. So she said, "Okay, if you think that it's best. But I am hungry right now, could you just get me something to eat? Chicken please! So he stood up and headed out for her meal. Shortly after that, they got to learn how to live together. They learned a lot about each other and yet still managed to get along. As time passed by, Tahoe was now seven months pregnant. So now was the time that her man felt that they were ready to move to Washington, D.C. and they packed up all they had, loaded up the SUV and hit the road. The driving was not bad at all because the SUV had lots of room and it was a comfortable ride. They drove for about two and a half days on the road making good time on the highway. Well, by the time they arrived in Washington, D.C, Tahoe started to have labor pains. Her man knew he had no choice but to get her to D.C. General Hospital as fast as he could. This came as a complete surprise to them both because the baby had at least two months before it was due. Well, **obviously,** the baby had a change of heart 'cause as soon as Tahoe arrived at the hospital, the baby was on his way. This was a very stressful situation for her man because he was a fugitive wanted by the law. With that being said, he had to lay low, off the radar due to the nature of his kind of work. He could not be on the scene with law enforcement, police, ambulances, security guards, etc., all these type people made him extremely nervous. **He knew that there were warrants out for his arrest for the past six months or so for drug trafficking, money laundering, and weapons.** He was also aware of the fact that the police had been hot on his trail down in Louisana, but he had been lucky so far. And he would like to keep it that way. So after, little Jimmy was born, he managed to get a picture taken for himself of his baby boy. After that, he planted a roll of money underneath Tahoe's pillow, and solemnly kissed her good bye. To this day, she has never heard from him again. Tahoe was glad her baby boy was fine, just like his dad. Her first thought was that this would really be a special Christmas for me. But then, Tahoe thought to herself again. I cannot believe this is for real. Here I go again. I am in this strange city far away from home. And I have been abandon once again. **Again. there lies another legacy of abandonment for a black family to overcome.** So, at that point, Tahoe prayed for strength and held her baby boy tight. She refused to abandon her child, 'cause she knew that she was all that her baby boy had. Tahoe did go through a rough time, but God answered her prayers. She made it though with God's help. She finally realized that she needed to accept the fact that living in this strange city was an anomaly, but that it was now her adopted home. The wayward path of an exceptionally bright young man is a testimony of the life and journey of Jimmy Black. But what comes to play most significantly right now is the fact that Jimmy Black is a grown man. Tahoe is aware that Jimmy has many of his dad's ways, but that he is a genuinely good man. This is what makes Tahoe the most proud. It's simply the fact that her son is a good man. And God stuck by her side and blessed her every day, helping her to raise her child to be a good man. Jimmy Black Blango was now eighteen years old. He now had four siblings as well. in fact, Tahoe Blango has five children all together. They are doing fairly well, living in the heart of the projects in S.E., Washington, D.C.

Today at work was weird. We all went throughout the morning with our routine daily activities. Then, about lunch time, we were all informed by our supervisor, Mr. **Baukworth** that he had scheduled a mandatory meeting at 2:00 p.m. Now, by virtue of the fact that today was a Friday, and we all wanted out of there on time. We knew how crazy that commute could be on Friday evenings. And the majority of our staff at the prison lived on the other side of the bridge in Washington D.C. or Maryland with family members depending on our contributions. During a brief moment of contemplation, as we were all seated in the conference room, waiting for the other colleagues to arrive, we discussed the current gossip and rancor of the day. Now aside from getting the latest news about, the lieutenants, officers, and managers that are having extramarital affairs, we moved the subject matter along to a far more pressing topic as well. We knew that everyone was aware of the anticipated closure of the Lorton Complex. So with President Bill Clinton's proclamation being signed into law. **The national capital revitalization and self-government improvement act of 1997**, which constituted the final nail in the coffin for the Lorton Complex. The next topic on the hot plate was the most anticipated, dreaded, controversial discussion, better known to all as the "reduction-in-force (RIF)" topic. There have been so many rumors about whose name was on the list, why certain staff members were never put on the list, and how were some names skipped over others, and how did it happen that some names were suddenly removed? Then, more importantly, who might be the next person on that list to loose their job. Supposedly, all of this information came from the D.C. Office of Personnel Management. With that being said, this list was a confidential document and it was not supposed to be disseminated department-wide for everyone in the agency to peruse. But the Department of Correction's handling of that directive was a fiasco. But this was not at all that strange coming from the corruption and distortion that breeds from this department on a regular basis.

Now, Jimmy Black and has friends grew up together in the low-income housing projects of S.E. Washington, D.C. Basically, Jimmy Black and his crew were close. They were as thick as thieves. They spent nights together, they went to school together, played sports together, they did almost everything together. It became evident that judging from the character range of the crew, Jimmy Black stood shoulders above the rest as a natural born leader. He was charismatic, smart, handsome, and intelligent. He also knew that he had possessed an exceptionally kin, sharp, brutal mind. His class work in school absolutely baffled his teachers. Even at an early age, he struggled to hone in on these abilities, i.e., talents and channel them for the good of mankind, instead of profiteering from contributions being made for nefarious activities that lead to criminal activity. He has possessed the talent of photographic memory since elementary school. Teachers would always seem baffled or somewhat appalled when Jimmy Black would miss classes for weeks at a time, yet, return to class and preformed better than half the class that came every day. Quite frankly, some of his peers worked tentatively at their studies, and put extra efforts in their class assignments. Yet, they too were shocked at his ability grasp the class assignments without being challenged. So from time to time, Jimmy Black (JB) got tired of trying to explain, or offer an excuse for doing well. He just wished that the teachers would leave him alone and teach the most needy, who lacked the proficient skills. He cared less about what the other kids said about him. He could take the heat on his own. He just wasn't that good of a teacher personality type. He knew how he got the right answers and understood the concepts, but it was difficult for him to explain what he knew and to what extent he understood to others. In fact, to him, this education thing was always a fluid situation for him, it was constantly changing. Anyway, his aspiration were to some day leave the thug life behind and be a law-abiding citizen, but, for now the money was paying the bills and paying them pretty good. But he knew that there was a better life for him out there somewhere. You see, Jimmy Black better known by his peers as JB. Defied all the odds, this young Afro-American kid, haphazardly ripped through the academic platform of his junior high school without being challenged on his level.

Theoretically speaking, it has long been held as a fundamental truth that education was the key to what was lacking to bridge the gap between the rich and the poor. To prove the basis for this hypothesis, one can draw conclusions from this sample pilot study. This is not a scientific study, but, it can be utilized for generic purposes. Now, with the exception of Jimmy Black (JB), this study on its face value holds up overwhelmingly true. This particular study cites an example of two children from the opposite ends of the economic spectrum. First, we began the battery of test with the wealthy child whom has every asset at home that prepares him to excel academically at school. And his test results were extremely high. Again, this by the way, was not a surprise.

Secondly, the other child was from a low-income family home. This child enters and begins testing. This particular child was raised without the benefits of a nurturing home and lacked the preparations for standard test requirements when academically challenged. He did not perform on grade level.

So the test results for the poor child were not a surprise. As a matter of fact, this particular child failed all the test.

So if the overall outcome of the test results were no surprise, why do the school officials or even on a larger scale, why do society seem to wonder why is it that one child performs so much better than the other child? Yet we continue to hold all children to the same standards. Notwithstanding the fact that you can plainly see that they were not given the benefits of an equal playing field. With that being said, these test are not fair in the sense that they will be utilized by the school system for tracking purposes, end of grade testing/evaluations, IQ purposes, etc.

For it is without a doubt that the institution that separates their two worlds is the institution of poverty. Reportedly, there are approximately 46.2 million people or close to one in six people living in poverty in America, today. Quite frankly, tremendous gains could be made, within the grand scheme of things if some measures were taken in society as a whole to deal with the institution of poverty.

Generally speaking, most of the hypothesis cited above would be accepted in layman terms as a valid proposition, but it's not that readily accepted by the academic world. You see, simply because a child is poor, does not mean that that child lacks the potential/ability to learn. Now, at the end of the year, most of our third graders take what's called an end-of-grade (EOG) test, and that test is used to determine whether or not that child will be sent to the next grade or retained at his or her current grade level. This particular test does not take into account your socio-economic background or status. These are all statewide test and they are scored by state officials. Although it is unfortunate that some poor kids are without the resources that are afforded to the rich, they will still have to be tested by the same standardized test. And, yes, by the way, this is fair. Ultimately, what it comes down to is priorities. What I mean is that for the rich kid, his parents have a vested interest in their child's education and that child's learning is priority number one to both his parents. On the other hand, the poor kid, has no one with a vested interest in their academic future. He has one parent in the home, and that would his mother. Now, given all the different hats that she has to wear in the home, there's little time left for her to do the academics too. Not only that, she might not be able to perform on grade level herself. So priorities are very important in the home. It's important to take an interest in your child's education regardless of your socio-economic status. First, you can start by building up their vocabulary. For example: utilized environmental print, supermarket signs, letters, magazines, newspapers, library, TV screenings/ learning channels, computers, internet, etc. Again, it's all about priorities. The world won't alter its standards just because you are poor. And, one last point, if there are kids with challenges such as learning disabilities, along with Exceptional Handicaps (EH), or Exceptional Mental Handicap (EMC), and self contained/wheelchairs, etc., if they can still past their End-of-Grade (EOG) test, then what's the excuse for the poor child not passing his/her test?

Now, to recapture some of the background on Jimmy Black, it would be safe to say there has never been one word ever mentioned about his father, nor did he even know who his father was. He had four other siblings whom all had different fathers as well. Lord knows, it had never crossed his mind to ask what was his father's name. Jimmy often thought to himself, what difference does it make whether he knew his name or who he was, 'cause he would be eighteen years old on December 5 this year. So he figured he had made it this far without knowing his father, so why should he try to get to know him now.

Growing up in the streets of Washington, D.C. was not easy. Man, I have heard older dudes say that once upon a time, D.C. was called chocolate city, simply because back in the '80s, there were more black people per capital square mile living in the nation's capital than any other of the fifty states in America. Hell, that's something to think about, I wasn't even born. Well, just look at how times have change. Jimmy dropped out of school at the age of fifteen primarily due to being caught up by the Metropolitan Police Department making an arrest. But when Tahoe found that out, she wasn't having that and she put that little black ass right back in school. He might have repeated at least one year, but his mom made him go right back to school. After being in and out of jail for the last couple of years, time slipped away real fast. It was like, hey, I'm 'bout to be eighteen years old out here for real. It was a miracle from God that that little hoodlum graduated, but he did. From there, he thought to himself, I need to start making real big man choices, 'cause I'm the real deal now. But on one of those scenes with the police, he was high and things got a little out of hand, and everything was just off the chang. This scene was just crazy. Jimmy explained his account of the incident as follows: I took a volunteer position at a bowling alley, in order to try to build up my drug clientele. So business was zooming. but I made the mistake of allowing a sample of my K2 stash to get into the hands of a meth-head, better known as a D.C. upper class suburbanite. This white kid was a topflight, first class druggie. This freak didn't even ask what I had, he just raised up on me, and swallowed before I could blink. From there, things just got out of hand. First, he started to foam at the mouth. That's when one dude called 911. At that point, the pit of his eyes turned into **the color of a jewellike** iridescent and, then off came his clothes. Shortly after that, he just ran around in circles like his ass was on fire until the police came. Man, he couldn't even talk. Whenever he opened his mouth to say a word, no sound came out. His voice was gone. By that time, the ambulance was on the scene. I made sure I stayed far enough from harm's way so the po po couldn't see me. Hell, I won't going to jail for no damn K2. So that's all I have to say about that and that's that. With that being said, **God knows that that scene was just crazy.** And Jimmy Black left that bowling alley on that particular occasion, with the contention that everything was just too crazy. But from that scene, he came upon another. on this last beef, this one right here, really didn't make no sense. Man, for the last couple of years, I've been trying to turn over a new leaf and change my ways, 'cause I'm getting older now man, I got to step up and make some changes. This is for real, man. This police game is just whack, man, I got to do better, man. Well, to start with, the police done gone crazy as hell, I mean it, man, they locking up everything. Man, this one police that I sell my dope to even tried to turn on me, and lock my black ass up, until, I snitched on another niggar. Man, they clean, sweeping every niggar on the street. Man, half the northeast crew in D.C. Lincoln Heights got locked up by operation clean sweep (undercover police). Man, I swear man, the police are haters, man, they haters. I just believe that they hate the black man 'cause we are the ones that sale their sons and daughters all their dope and we get to take all their money, man. So they just want to get even by sending all of us to jail. And they own the court system, so they make sure we go to jail and stay a long, extra long time. But man, I ain't going down like that man. Man, I done did that Lorton thing, man. Hell naw, I don't wanna go back. But this is what I'm trying to say. First of all, 'cause so many of us drug dealers were getting locked up, we decided to lay low, or go underground for awhile, until the police cooled off the streets. So our next move was to take on another hustle in order to supplement the income from the drug sales. We decided to do this warehouse heist to get all the top of line collectable Nike tennis shoes. Now, this brother up the street from where we lived, worked at the Nike shoe outlet. And I decided that he was the dude that we would use to help set up the heist. I targeted mike to help setup the heist 'cause his girlfriend was Shannon, yet, I caught him getting his groove on with Alicia. I never interrupted them, I just waited until they got through and then made my presence known. He knew when in told him about the heist that I would tell Shannon about his little affair if he refused to comply. So he had no choice but to comply. Anyway, the stupid niggro didn't even have much to do. By the way, we planned for the whole thing to take place while his manager was on vacation. But anyway, all I wanted him to do was what he normally does. I told him to go on his break, and prior to his return, go to the back door, leading to the loading docks, and leave the back door ajar, so we could get in. From there, he could use whatever prop he wanted to use. That was his choice. Well, after he did his part, at least we had access. Now, when I say we, I mean me and my crew, I MEAN MY HOME BOYS. Man, me and my dogs, we been scrapping out here a long time. We go way back to elementary school. Man, you can't beat that. Well, anyway, it was me, Cecil Sutton, Marlow McCoy and Larmar Taylor. I did my part right 'cause I hotwired the truck over in S.E. So all of us got into the truck and drove to the warehouse over to Southeast Benning Rd., and pulled up behind the loading docks. The loading docks were adjacent to a huge cadre of burly, thick cheney bushes that mounted alongside the loading docks. And when we got there everything looked good. We saw the stick in the door where Mike used to keep it propped open for us. So we went inside the warehouse. Man, this place was huge. There was one small florescent light in each corner of the warehouse. We saw boxes that were stacked up against all four walls. So we had enough light to do what we came to do. It was about 9:30 p.m., when we arrived. Now, when we first arrived, I began to voice my opinion about the whole thing. SO, I SAID, "Look here, y'all, I ain't no big fan of this HERE type of gig. This here just really ain't my thing. I'm a drug man."

Really, that's what I do, man, I'm a drug dealer. Then, Marlow cut his eyes sharp back at me and said, "Man, y'all niggars need to shut the hell up. Let's just get this shit and get out of here." So with that being said, Ce and Larmar began to grab boxes and started stacking them on a dollie. So, when the merchandise was secured, they both scrapped the bundles on top of the dollies. When it was full to the top, they pushed it outside, wheeled them behind the huge rows of cheney bushes, and loaded the boxes in the back of the stolen truck. Then, after that first load, I said to myself, "Hey, know what? That wasn't so bad. But what I do know is that we all better start getting jiggy with it." Then, the next thing I know, I'm telling them to hustle, hustle, move it, go faster, faster, so we can get the hell out of here. Well, at that point, everybody started moving faster. And it did seem like the operation was speeding up. And before too long we were all loaded up and ready to go. Now, we had made a clean getaway. The merchandise was fresh off the chain too. We were all loaded up on our way back from the hood, when just one block away, we got stopped by the damn po-po. Man, that's some fucked up crackhead move right there. Man, I just hung my head low. Then, without saying one word, I just slowed down, pumped my breaks and pulled that gear into park. As soon as I heard the siren, I knew what was up. I just wanted that po-po to do his damn thing, and let us go the hell on. Well, that sho didn't turn out like I hoped. Next thing I saw, there's was about fifty po-po cars surrounding the truck and we all sitting inside looking stupid, stupid as hell. They had swat teams, bomb squads, FBI Drug interdiction Units, Canine units, etc. Man, they rolled up on us with their guns blazing. They acted like we were on the scene of America's Most Wanted hosted by John Walsh or some type of damn Benghazi terrorist attack squad, straight out of Libya, or something like that damn FT. HOOD ARMY SNIPER ATTACK in Texas. Anyway, we all got arrested and sent to the D.C. jail. Man, that was the saddest day of my life. For real, man, that was the saddest day of my life.

Meanwhile, this jail cell is a beast. Man, it's brutal on the mind. The complete audacity of the humane mind is a book all by itself. No, let me rephrase that, it's a whole damn world all by itself. I'm sitting here 'bout to lose my damn mind, trying to keep the sanity of my mind. I often contemplate the plight of my current situation. The whole scene keeps playing itself out over and over in my head. And it's just not adding up. Somebody had to tip the police off. Man, it was too calibrated, nothing spontaneous generated from the A-Z. Man, we got hoodwinked, bamboozled, jacked, or whatever. It is hard as hell being locked up behind these bars. Man, you got to be strong to do a bid like this every single day. This whole jail shit is just crazy. Man, this here is a damn crazy place for real. Man, when you lose your freedom, you lose so much. You lose your pride, your dignity, your contact with humanity, and I can go one-step further than that, hell, you lose the feel of human touch. From there, you get confused when you encounter emotions or feelings. Most of the time, your reactions are faked instead of being real spontaneous and genuine. They are that way because after being away from human contact for so long, you are left empty, void of the ability to feel, or gage the appropriate humane instinct. And most of the time you try to mimic the emotion that you see, hoping that it's the right choice. So you need time once you get released to learn how to re-access the basics in human emotions. Then there's the most important human instinct of all, the ability to love. Well, that's another emotion that one could never find enough words to capture the true essence of. Quite frankly, I would venture to say that there are simply not enough **WORDS ON PLANET EARTH THAT COULD assimilate the chemistry of love.** Well, I sure have had my bouts with the ladylove and she is not to be played. I tell you what, I played ladylove one time too many and I learnt my lesson. I won't be playing that game no more. So when I found my Boo, I was happy. I've been with my Boo since we met. We've been together for about three years now. Okay, I just found out about my baby girl two weeks before we got caught up in this heist thing. Man, it really freaked me out, 'cause the first thing I said was, it ain't mine. Then I felt bad 'cause I hurt her feelings. I knew that shorty is my Boo and she wouldn't do no shit like that behind my back. So I came back and fixed that shit up real good. So she's smart. She got DNA test and that baby girl is mine. Only thing though, I never got the chance to tell my mom, Tahoe, 'cause they locked me up. Man, telling my mom that I got a baby girl, my first and my only child is the last thing I wanted to do, hanging from a jail cell. Yeah, I'm facing three-to-nine years on a tech violation, plus a brand new twenty-five to thirty years for these charges on this new arrest, man, this shit right here is whacked. Man, that's way too much time, man. I just can't help but feel like that something just don't add up. Man, sooner or later, it will all shake out. But watch what I say, something funny 'bout how all that went down. Man, this psychology thing man, like I said all of these thoughts are playing **foosball in my mind.** I tell you what man, long as I can maintain without a nervous breakdown or some type of DAMN psychotic episode, I'll be all right, but this jail cell will make you psychotic if you let it. So there, Jimmy Black sits in his jail cell all alone. This is the most brutal, cold, and inhumane place on earth. I mean the bond goes deep amongst friends and that's how me and my crew rolled. My fond memories of our friendship and the bond that we shared is all that keeps me together right now. Man, we don't do no snitching, so all of that is for them fake niggars and we for real. So we all gonna make it out all right. Anyway, that big ass hole in the wall that they call a cell is about 9x5 cubic square feet. Man, it's barely enough room to turn around in here. I'm a big dude yo, and I need lots of room. As a matter of fact, it's not enough air to breathe in here, I hate small places. I like large places. Hell, I like large everything. Now, I'm just sitting here thinking, how am I gonna make this raggedy, shagged frail iron framed box magically transform itself into a bunk to fit me? Man, as soon as you walk into the cell, you see attached to the wall are two small shanty style bunk beds made of multiple slabs of coil wires stretched along horizontal rows from head to toe on a small iron frame with no mattress. The bottom bunk is raised about two (2) feet off the floor. Consequently, there is limited headroom left at the top bunk. On the other hand, depending on your height there WOULD BE limited space for the bottom bunk as well. It is significant to note that JAIL SPACE is always limited space, and THAT'S ALL DAY, EVERY DAY at the Lorton prison. Now, depending the location of your cell, and given four walls, its designed to have three sides of the walls with bars and one concrete wall which contains just enough space for the two small bunk beds. In prison, real estate is a hot commodity. Therefore, all room and/or space is a prized possession. Remember, in jail, there's always limited space for everything. Anyway, the floors are usually made of concrete with one toilet at the foot area of the small bunk beds. Then, the sink is more or less something like a contraption straight out of some star wars marathon revealing the dynamic features of multitasking for alien drones. Once again, in essence, this foreign object called a sink appeared to be a stainless steel round bowl (4 feet), mounted to a concrete cement obelisk cinder block. The cell also has two vertical style wall lockers with combination locks which is located at the head area of the bed bunks. There's almost never any privacy. But I truly think that they designed that shit to be that way on purpose. Be that as it may, I'm just lucky right now that I don't have a roommate. I'm just here by myself right now. But anyway, the view on almost every wall in this place lacks contour lines, shapes, and its colorless or void of texture. Believe it or not, the eyes can get so tired overtime of the soft-grained etching of obscure black and white **concrete** that the brain will puke at first sight. I just hope I'm not here that long. Not only is this place bad on your eyes, it's bad for your health. Man, I've heard that some dudes have been locked up in here so long that they have literally lost their minds. Some prison stories that go past these prison cells are just crazy. Man, we just heard the other day that some prison out in California blew a hole in the count for three days. It took the prison officials three days before they could determine why the count would not clear. Upon investigation, it was determined that one inmate allegedly murdered his cell-mate. Then, he ate his cell-mate and almost got away with it, until the prison officials were unable to clear a formal count. Man, this dude was another Jeffery Dahmer. Remember, that Jeffery Dahmer was the serial killer that brutally murdered his victims and later dismembered their bodies. Then, he would refrigerate their organs, save them, and periodically cooked them for his meals. So man you got a lot of mental health patients locked up in prison. Aside from that issue, man, the air is just outright brazenly, stale, cold, and dry. Really, half the time it's polluted with stench so foul that it curls the rib cage at the pit of its core. The frequent smell of expelled gas is seemingly so foul, it burns the hairs off the canal of the nose. On the other hand, if you can acquiesce that moment in time, then you can appreciate the significance of every company that manufactures breathe mints, mouthwash, air fresheners, deodorants, soaps, etc. Speaking of bad breath by the way, at certain times in the morning and throughout much of the noonday, the air can be considered by the Department of Defense to what's equivalent to WEAPONS OF MASS DESTRUCTION or (lethal) chemical weapon, similar to a stash of nerve gas that is hoist by Syria, Iraq or Iran. Man, some dudes breath is equivalent to toxic putrid gas that pollutes the air. Man, when some of these guys wake up in the morning, their breath is so bad it's beyond halitosis, I declare it is. IT'S LIKE THE CITY DUMP OR NEIGHBORHOOD LANDFILL. And I'm tired of all these chains, I feel like a caged animal. I'm tired of these bars. I know that most of this is about mind games. But I do know that these mind games can run amok and take you over the edge if left unchecked. But it's just frustrating that whenever I move, I'm in the three-piece suit. I'm in hand cuffs, leg irons, a belly chain, and black box like I'm Hannibal or some masked murderer. Man, I'm ready to move away from this jail. This is nothing but pure hell. I'm hoping I can get gone soon too.

JIMMY ANTICIPATES A NEW MOVE

WELL, I TELL YOU WHAT, HUSTLING DOWN AT LORTON was HARD AS HELL. I spent about four to five months at the D.C. Jail before I got shipped to Lorton. For the most part, I was glad too, 'cause I was tired of that jail for real 'cause it was just too tight. What I meant was that it was hard to roam around at that jail because they had controlled movement. In other words, all of your movements preempted a tentatively targeted protocol that generated the need for YOUR NEXT movement. Hence, random movements were few and far between. If you were not authorized or had permission to do so, you could not move. And the Department of Corrections had never forgotten that July 10, 1986, prison disturbance at the Occoquan Facility which caused them a full-blown media frenzy. Not to mention a major three-alarm fire which cost the city millions, and prompted the bids for prison contracts throughout the United States. So stop gap measures were put into place to avoid mistakes repeated from the past.

Certain requirements for the superintendents were NOW BEING PUT IN to PLACE TO **flag all measures that alerts alarming activity** in the areas such as:

Excessive inmate's movements
Facilities that dismiss overcrowding measures
Troubleshooting contract facilities for emergency transfers
Excessive Gang related activities
Employee/Inmate high profile drug surveillance activity, etc.
Workplace violence and harassment
Employee/Inmate sexual harassment
Excessive violent assaults/alerts from random siren alarms

Upon these notations being flagged, they had to be reported within twenty-four hours To the director of the Department Of Corrections, whereas further determinations were then being made by a higher authority on the agency's behalf.

From there, the doc officials wanted to be proactive whenever possible instead of having to be reactive in crisis management mode on a status quo basis. Therefore, they wanted to no longer conduct business as usual within the department of corrections. They were now being grafted into the Federal Bureau of Prisons due to the **National Capital Revitalizational and Reorganization Act of 1997** and they knew that they had an image problem that badly needed repair. And to try to get ahead of some of the media bliss before the closure transformation took hold would not hurt at all. So you could see where residual changes were being made, and how that continuing these measures would become the new norm for the D.C. Department of Corrections.

Well, as far as Jimmy Black could tell, his journey was right on track. And he continues to explain all of the encounters at Lorton as apart of doing time. So he explained this particular experience like this. Although apprehensive, I knew ahead of time that my transfer to Lorton was eminent. Anyway, I had my ways of being resourceful. Besides that, I knew a few people in high places. So I put in a bid to see, the superintendent first before I left, just to get the show on the road. You see, I wanted to be fully equipped to start my hustle when I got to Lorton. First, I got this work squad detail. And this had proven to be a great asset to my hustle down at Lorton. Some inmates worked as ground maintenance or landscaping crew. This essentially was rich proving ground for transporting contraband. Man, I got hired for work squad by Bobby Jennings. And I needed this work squad to run my game. I was good with that quick move too, 'cause I've known Bobby since junior high school. As a matter of fact, we graduated from Ballou High School in S.E. Washington, D.C, back in 2001. Now, most of the routes along that detail for work squad, I already knew, so my peeps had already laid my stash out for me. Now, this is a true bill, believe it when I tell you, this is real as real can be. Listen up, man, our work squad crews were never searched upon their return to the facility. This was good news to us because at that point, we had open assess to the movement of the merchandise that we had to sell throughout the compound. This was literally an open-air drug market. Aside from all that, the schedule that I had laid out for myself was fierce. This is how I set my schedule up. I was assigned to work squad on Mondays and Tuesdays. So we had to report for work early on early on Mondays and Tuesdays around 5:30 a.m., and we didn't get back to Lorton until after 5:00 p.m. Then, on Wednesdays and Thursdays, I worked in the chapel from 9:00 a.m.-5:00 p.m. as the choir director. Then, on Fridays, I had free time to play catch up on last minute deals that never got processed. In other words, somebody dropped the ball. So I had to step in and close the deal. Usually, I was busy all week. But our team, we worked well together. Hell, what can I say? I ran a smooth operation. Man, the money was sho 'nuf cranking out there. We show got paid, every day. So let me start over at the beginning. See, it's not hard to get locked up in Washington, D.C, my hometown. But really, it's probably not hard to get locked up anywhere in this united states especially for DWB (driving while black) or WWB (walking while black). The United States incarcerate more people in America than any industrial nation in the world. With that being said, the largest percentage of the ethnic population currently incarcerated is Afro-Americans. Yet, they only make up approximately 16.2% of the total population. Anyway, when you get locked up in the district you are S-U-B-J-E-C-T-E-D to being simply harassed. For the most part, the criminal justice system can be an intimidating experience. The process itself includes every encounter that an individual experiences from arrest through prosecution and conviction to the final stages of release from commitment. There are also conditions whereby freedom can be obtained during certain stages of this process. In fact, prosecutors on occasions may drop cases due to lack of evidence, mistaken identity, plea bargaining, civil rights violations, etc. The criminal justice process in the District of Columbia is one example of how numerous agencies work together to process individuals through the criminal justice system (see attached chart). This list of agencies include the following:

1. Metropolitan Police Department
2. Pretrial Service Agency
3. United States Attorney General's Office
4. United States Attorney's Office
5. United States Marshals Service
6. Superior Court of the District of Columbia
7. United States District Court / District of Columbia
8. The Legal Assistance Branch of the D.C. Superior Court
9. District of Columbia Probation Departments
10. Court Services and Offender Supervision Agency
11. United States Probation Department
12. Public Defender Service
13. Office of Corporation Counsel
14. D.C. Department of Corrections
15. D.C. Parole Board
16. Federal Bureau of Prisons
17. United States Parole Commission

WALKING THROUGH THE DISTRICT OF COLUMBIA'S CRIMINAL JUSTICE SYSTEM CAROLYN WILLIAMS

LEAD AGENCY	Arrest	Booking	Indictment	Arraigment	Prelimenary Hearing	Detention	Conviction	Sentence	Commitment
Metro Police	X	X							
Pre-trial Agency	X	X	X	X	X	X			
U.S. Attorney General Office			X	X	X	X	X		
ILS. Marshall Service						X			
D.C. Superior Court							X	X	
U.S. District Court							X	X	
Legal Asst. Branch							X	X	
D.C./U.S. Probation Dept.							X	X	X
Public Defender Service			X	X	X	X	X	X	
Office of Corporation Counsel							X	X	
D.C. Dept. of Corrections									X
Federal Bureau of Prisons									X
D.C. Parole Board									X

Please note that the mark of [x] next to the agency indicates that a significant role was played in the corresponding stage of the criminal justice process.

When an individual is taken into custody by the police and detained (deprived of liberty by legal authority) for violating the law, he is considered to be **under arrest.**

As we can account for the incident that sent Jimmy Black and his crew to jail, it was quite an eye opening experience to say the least. In recalling the events of this particular scene, the boys were removed from the stolen truck driven by Jimmy with Lamar riding shotgun, while both Cecil and Marlow were seated in the back. The D.C. Police were brazen in their tactical five-point stealth plan for takedown. The scene was a textbook format operation. And Washington, D.C. has always been known for being the most well versed law enforcement jurisdiction in the country. So the District, they just made use of those resources while showing off a formidable display of force for the 11:00 evening news. In less than forty minutes, all four suspects were in custody, arrested, and booked within the D.C. Department of Corrections.

Now, we know most of the turmoil within the Tahoe Blango family centers on the issue of abandonment. Yet, here again we have the issue of Jimmy being locked up and separated from his new born baby girl, not to mention members of his own family. Now, this really hurt his mom, Tahoe, who in so many ways counted on Jimmy as the head of household. She depended on him for financial resources that subsidized the welfare of their family. Although Tahoe received public assistance, food stamps, and low-income housing, she would often fall on hard times, and needed extra funds just to get by. Now, that's when Jimmy Black stepped in and provided the help she needed. So for that resource alone, his mom would truly miss out on her son's help. But aside from all of that, Tahoe missed her son. She had been heartbroken since being told that he was locked up at Lorton. Remember, Tahoe still had four other children at home to feed. So she felt she had to stay strong for them too, at least until Jimmy came home.

Well, when I first got arrested, I waited awhile before I called home 'cause I thought I would get things to work out for me and I could make it home before mom would ever find out. But, naw man, I had this court appointed pencil pushing dweeb, who just was an a-hole. Man, that **Mr. Alex Hershel** show put a hurting on my ass. I just knew I could plead out this case until he kept playing that bluffing game with the United States Attorney. Shit, man that damn rookie cost me my freedom. I could have made it home with that damn plea. Oh, hell, it's hard but it's fair. Beside that man, I ain't no snitch, so I won't going to trial no matter what. You see, me and my dogs, we don't roll like that. Now, Jimmy and his road dogs were not strangers to the system. They were doing drive-bys at the **po po (slang for police)** since junior high school. In other words, this ain't Jimmy's first rodeo. Their charges were mainly drug related and petty theft. But their wrap sheets were quite extensive to say the least, as TALL as THE DAY IS LONG. Anyway, the Mayor, **Mr. Juan Freeman** was up for reelection and didn't want to appear to be soft on crime. Needless to say, the city was determined to get their pound of flesh. And that meant that if you were labeled a career criminal in this political climate, then you are probably going to do time in jail period.

So after an arrest, the accused usually encounters a process called **booking** at the police station. Booking means that police officers will make a formal police report that documents the arrest. This report will usually require that the accused be subjected to fingerprints and photographs or mug shots. And from what we could tell in this case, they did. Nevertheless, it is significant to note that the Fifth Amendment of the United States constitution provides citizens with the right against self-incrimination. Therefore, the accused has the right to remain silent. This means that the accused cannot be forced to testify against him or herself. Therefore, the police are required to inform the accused of their Miranda rights when making an arrest. The Miranda rights reads as follows:

1. You have the right to remain silent. Anything you say can be used against you in a court of law.
2. You have a right to have a lawyer and to have one present while you are being questioned.
3. If you cannot afford a lawyer, one will be appointed for you before questioning begins. (1)

Arbetman, O'Brien, McMahon, *Street Law,* (United States: West Publishing Company, 1990) p. 109.

Rush, Jeffery, _Probation Officer/Parole Office Exam_. (United States: Thomson Learning Inc, 2000).

Ryan, Daniel, Pretrial Release and Detention., Washington, D.C. Administrative Office of United States Courts, 1993.

From there, they were arraigned in Superior Court by **Judge August Greene.** But they each had separate court appearances. In the case of Jimmy Black, the court appointed attorney, Mr. Alex Hershel, initially spoke to the judge in an effort to request from the district attorney that a plea deal be part of the negotiations that were brought to the table on his behalf. Nevertheless, at the preliminary hearing, the judge wanted at least a pound of flesh or some jail time due to the seriousness of the charges in the case i.e., robbery, attempted robbery, (breaking and entering), unauthorized use of a vehicle, unauthorized possession of a stolen vehicle, and possession of a controlled substance (two counts), marijuana. However, the judge was especially impressed by the fact that Jimmy Black was able to follow instructions given by D.C Police and stop the vehicle. Heretofore, avoiding additional criminal charges, any high-speed chases, or perhaps the loss of life. Again, it took a tremendous amount of humility, good character, and fortitude to stop on a dime to make a turn around, once the wheels are turning in the opposite direction. As far as the judge was concerned, these were the reasons for any leverage given for any sort of deal in the first place. But Mr. Hershel refused to compromise. He maintained that he would go with the plea deal, only if all the charges were dropped, he wanted credit for time served, no probation revocation, and demanded immediate release. On the other hand, the judge wanted more of a balanced deal (as a gesture of good faith) to be brought to bear and she scoffed at the notion of no jail time. And she refused to roll over on the revocation of probation deal which called for an immediate three to nine years. Now, at that point, I was okay with that deal. I would take the plea and finish that little time out for six months, probably? Finally, the district attorney took the deal off the table. Now, I'm the cooked goose. But that damn Mr. Hershel just couldn't leave well enough alone. That damn rookie got to learn when it's time to hold them and when it's time to fold them. Either way, I'm stuck here doing this time. Hell, I got three to nine years out this damn deal, but it could have been worst. Man, I'm doing time behind his ass. He pissed that judge off. Oh well, I just thank God that it wasn't too bad. Anyway, I refused to go to trial. I thank God too that I could still see the light of day. And hopefully, enjoy my little girl while she was still small. So it was still a blessing. I talked with my mom, Tahoe, she fasted and prayed for me too. So I know that whole deal came from God. Thank God for his grace and mercy. My case was over. So at the end of the day, I stated for the record with a clear conscience, "Hell, I'll take a deal for the three to nine years, Alex! And finally, that whole matter was adjourned.

Now, as previously mentioned, at an **Arraignment phase**, the accused person is brought before a judge where the charges are read aloud before the accused. At some point, the accused will be asked whether or not he/she will be represented by his/her own attorney or would he/she will be requesting a court appointed attorney. Also, the question will be asked whether he/she will be pleading guilty or not guilty. Then, in closing the proceeding will address the issue of **bail.** It is significant to note that the Eighth Amendment of the constitution protects the accused from excessive bail, but it does not guarantee the right to bail. The main idea behind the concept of bail is to make sure that the accused returns to court for trial. Bail means that the accused will be ordered to pay 10% of the total payment that the court ordered for bail before he can be released. Finally, the issue of future court dates will be set up and the accused made fully aware of next court proceedings. From there, the court would then open the door for the next round of hearings scheduled for their docket. And this next set of hearings would address issues left unresolved from previous hearings, yet, move forward on matters involved at the **preliminary hearings** as well. Be advised that if the prosecutor finds **sufficient_probable cause** to issue an indictment than the information will be filed at the preliminary hearing. Shortly after that, the next court date scheduled for the accused will be set for trial. If found guilty of a felony offense in a court of law and ordered to serve time in Washington, D.C., the accused will be turned over to the custody of the United States Attorney General.

However, the paramount issue that continued to plague the D.C. Officials and completely paralyzed the prison operations at the Lorton Complex was massive overcrowding. Perhaps there was some ominous scheme that had been perpetrated by the news media or perhaps not. Yet, the evidence was hard to refute. Either way, something had to be done right away. At some point, in 1995, almost every Lorton prison was overcrowded. Much of this activity exploded on the heels of the crack cocaine epidemic (1995-1996) that literally had a domino effect whereby one agency's plight had an adverse effect on another. The scenario that played itself in this manner was primarily due to the fact that the agencies themselves were interdependent to each other. Yet, despite of the law that mandated Lorton closure by congress in 2001, the issue of overcrowding remained prevalent throughout (i.e., from 1994-1999), hence, this stymied much of the transition process. Consequently, it became evident that the way forward demanded that the revolving doors serving to perpetuate the onslaught of overcrowding permanently be closed. Therefore, in moving forward, no progress could be made without attention being solely directed toward solutions that addresses the problem of overcrowding.

Being processed through the criminal justice system does not always have to result in the service of a prison term. There are numerous programs which can provide the offender with alternatives to detention. This same scenario played itself out in Jimmy's Black case as well. Only thing though, he didn't need the bail hearings due to the fact that his probation violation was an automatic return to jail deal. In fact, Jimmy Black had been processed through the criminal justice system on many occasions. He had even served a couple jail terms at Lorton before. On both counts, they were drug charges. But those experiences taught him how to survive out there on the streets of Washington, D.C. With that being said, he begin practicing the tricks of his trade by discovering new tools for his drug market while confined at Lorton. But he vowed never to come back until this last crack head move that got him and his crew locked up. That's right, remember that stupid heist with the Nike tennis shoes. Although, waking up finding himself back in a jail cell was a reality check, he had to accept it and move on. In other words, count this experience as a lesson learnt from his past mistakes and keep moving forward. For the record, the Lorton that existed some twenty-five to thirty years ago was very much different from the Lorton that I am serving my time in today. Man, there are so many stories and folklores about the life and times from the Lorton Reservation that was passed on to us as kids, I couldn't even count them all. Oftentimes, we referred to the pastime stories that happened to be escapades about Lorton as tales from the hood. One example was about all of the violent murders, assaults, and stabbings that were generated by gang warfare, over drug turf, drug money, soliciting, prostitution, bribery, robbery, etc., all played themselves out at the Lorton Reservation. And the old folklore had always maintained that whenever you heard the glaring siren blasting high pitched with a loud shrieking horn throughout the reservation, you knew the somebody had just got stabbed. That noise was always followed by the high-speed ambulance paramedics chase and/or an emergency medical service squad careening up the highway from Fairfax County to the Lorton Complex to transport the injured. If the stabbing was severe or life threatening, and required immediate surgery, then you would hear the choppers in the air to medevac the injured out by helicopters to medical facilities with emergency trauma units on standby. Essentially, all emergency personnel on CALL FOR duty were our first line of defense for combating deadly violence at the Lorton Facilities. Sometimes, there would be two to three inmates with life threatening injuries. Unfortunately, there have been times whereby some expired. AGAIN, THESE WERE CAUSUALTIES OF prison warfare. But THIS was just one facet of the Lorton culture as a whole. Reportedly, the Lorton reservation was also known for being a work camp. They had many work squads that would start at the crack of dawn, worked a full day, and returned to the Lorton Reservation at the close of the business day. There were work squads for, dairy farm, agriculture, gardening, metal shop, clothing shop, mechanic work squad, chicken farms, etc. In fact, at some point they had farm animals of every kind (i.e., horse, cows, pigs, etc.). All of these work squads were readily available if not mandatory. **These work squads were open air markets for the transport of contraband throughout the Lorton Complex.** So, it has been said through old wise tales that the horse training work squad, along with the cow and dairy farm had proven to be some of the most popular work squads at Lorton. This was primarily because of the ease at which they had access to the heroin trade. The hay that was used to stock their stables was filled with straw that contained the drug. Early mornings they would pick up bales of hay to stock the horses/ cows stables. Then, after lunch, they would load the straws with heroin inside the truck and transport it back down to Lorton for sell and distribution. Another LORTON past time activity was making buck. This was what the inmate referred to as homemade wine.

Most of the homemade liquor was made in the work squads during the holiday season. Hell, we were told that the staff at the prison helped the inmates draw up the brew. It was also alleged that that the Green House planetarium not only grew garden vegetables, but cannabis sativa (marijuana) was a popular crop that grew on a small plot of land at the Lorton Reservation. Now, can you imagine that? Next on the list of traditions was an annual Lorton activity called Family Day. This was a big event every year at the Lorton Complex. It was a day set aside for drug dealers, gang bangers, and common criminals to take time off and called out a truce in order to enjoy some down time with family and friends. And enjoy they did. This was a day of fun for the kids, with lots of food, and drink. There were rides for the kids along with fun games and clowns. They had hot dogs, hamburgers, barbeque chicken, pork, potato salad, cold slaw, beans, ice cream, cookies, chips, iced tea, lemonade, etc. The inmates were allowed to have a minimum of two adult guest along with unlimited child admissions. This whole affair lasted all day. The inmates themselves provided their own entertainment for the adults. They used some of the instruments that were donated to the choir from prison outreach programs in the community. And the musicians in the prison choir volunteered their services to perform in the talent shows. It is significant to note that on one particular occasion (1995-1996), the inmates performed a new hit single by Tupac (legendary rap artist) called "Dear Mama." This performance received a standing ovation. It was very well received. These programs were very good for the inmate population, their families, and the surrounding community as well. There were also stories told about how those babies were being made on the Family Day at Lorton. This might be true to some extent because usually nine months after family day, the visiting hall would be half-full with brand new dads smoking small cigars or some brand of black and mild. And sure enough, there they would be holding little newborn babies. During the course of their visit, there would be lots of hugs and kisses, smiles and laughs, and tears of joy. Then, to save treasured memories of their time spent on that day, they would take several pictures. Usually, these were keepsake treasures for albums that would be past down to their kids.

Now, the work of pretrial services is very important in keeping the checks and balances within our jaded criminal justice system. Nevertheless, in most case, if the offender meets the minimum requirements for court-sponsored programs, it is highly probable that incarceration could be avoided all together. And with regard to the District of Columbia, they needed to avoid detention at all cost. In fact, President Ronald Reagan signed the Pretrial Services Act (18 U.S.C. Section 3152) into law on September 27, 1982. This particular legislation mandated that every judicial district establish a pretrial service program to work in conjunction with their court system. The mission of the pretrial service program is to make informed decision as it relates to how can justice best be served by meeting the needs of the individual without comprising the safety of the public? Ultimately, the goals and challenges faced by pretrial services are monumental in scope. Nevertheless, the organization has proven to be a tremendous asset to the judicial process. It has reaffirmed the notion of checks and balances within the scope of the criminal justice process. There are many duties and responsibilities of the pretrial service agency. In order to handle such a wide range of duties, the Parole/Probation Officers are often assigned to different sections within their divisions. Very often, the office has two separate sections for which staff members were assigned. Usually, those sections consist of investigation and supervision. To start with the investigation section, most of that arena consisted of the following: conducting interviews, prepare materials for court hearings, generates written formal reports, prepares presentence investigative report, and being responsible for the collection/verification of data. On the other hand, the supervision sections are primarily responsible for counseling individuals. They also are required to give notifications of court dates, processing bench warrants, issuance of supervision reporting notices, monitoring urine test results, monitoring pretrial diversion programs, and providing case management services. Keep in mind that all of these profound, duties and responsibilities are paramount to a well-balanced legal court system. As mentioned earlier, the information obtained by pretrial services comes from the interviews conducted by the Parole/Probation Officers. The initial interview is a crucial element of the data collection process because it provides the courts with vital information, which is then utilized to determine (case-by-case basis) appropriate decision regarding pretrial release and detention. For the most part, staff elicits extensive background data regarding the defendant's overall childhood experiences and lifestyle. This information contains data that involves family, marital status, community ties, citizenship, criminal background, employment history, medical history, mental health status, etc. Once the data is collected and verified, the staff prepares a formal report (i.e., presentence investigative report) which is then presented to the judge on behalf of the defendant. The presentence investigative report will be the instrument that helps the judge to determine his final course of action (release or detention) as it relates to the defendant's case. Also, keep in mind that all of the data presented to the judge in the presentence investigative report must be verified. Therefore, it is important that the agency conducts a formal investigation. Furthermore, pretrial service investigators have at their disposal many resources that allow them to verify data. In fact, back in the early 1990s, the Bureau of Prison Sentry System and the Probation and Pretrial Services Automated Case Tracking System (PACTS) are both Federal data bases that could verify data crucial to any investigation. Nevertheless, access to these systems requires authorization. But there are numerous government and private databases which can be accessed by pretrial service agencies as well. Moreover, each specific area has its own system established for the collection of data. Although the idea has been in the making for a while, consideration has be given to an integrated system of **Wide Area Networks** (WANS). and the **Local Area Networks** (LANS) which would then permit the officers to access data directly from their desk top computers. Again, these databases are authorized for the collection of data within specific areas only. In addition, this would allow information to be verified much quicker so that reports could be completed in a more timely fashion. Again, these databases are designated for a specific area Another area of responsibility within the office of pretrial services is that of supervision. In fact, the courts intermittently assign offenders to pretrial diversion programs, which specifically targets individuals eligible for release via program alternatives (e.g., halfway houses, substance abuse therapy, mental health therapy, vocational training, employment assistance, medical treatment, etc.). The pretrial diversion program selects individuals with little or no criminal background that poses no threat to thy community. Consequently, the successful completion of all program requirements grants the offender an opportunity to forego criminal prosecution and/or have all former charges filed in court dismissed. Therefore, this program is considered an incentive to the novice offender whom perhaps made a mistake and wants to avoid a future lifestyle of criminal activity. Additionally, the individuals selected for court-sponsored programs require supervision. The officers are required to supervise offenders that have been conditionally released on probation by the courts. Again, some areas of supervision are the monitoring of programs referrals. This area becomes evident whenever the courts institutes drug screening programs for cases that involve drug activity.

Therefore, when given access to the specifics of such data, officers will then screen the offenders that are court ordered for narcotics testing and/or treatment. If treatment referrals are a part of the court-ordered requirements, then contacts with program coordinators will be made. From there, placement would be swift and compliance mandatory. For the most part, probation officers are assigned numerous other duties as well. They write reports for the judges at the courts, conduct electronic surveillance, perform investigative functions, and they provide program services and/or treatments as mandated by the courts. Consequently, there will be cases that require the offender to report to his or her probation officer regularly as mandated by the courts or **vice versa** requires the probation officer will go visit the offender. In fact, given the bases from which to establish contact, there will be garnered a wealth of valuable intelligence from both parties to exchange. Quite frankly, it is standard procedure to set up a meeting with the offender to verify conditions established by the courts. As duly noted, the officer will conduct follow up interviews with employers, relatives, and friends regarding all social and work related activities. It is significant to note that new technology has allowed offenders to be tested more quickly, and have their results returned promptly without waiting for them to be sent to labs. In fact, many states have equipped their officers with portable breathalyzer units, on site drug testing materials, and various forms of disposable testing apparatus for alcohol/drug testing. These methods permit the officers to ascertain rapid results, which in turn provided the offenders with the proper treatment services needed in a timely manner. All of the efforts sought by the courts are truly welcomed by the district to stem the tide of massive prison overcrowding. Reportedly, in 1986, the District of Columbia implemented a well-established comprehensive drug-testing program. This program was brought about in Washington, D.C. due the efforts of the courts to reduce **prison overcrowding**, specifically pretrial incarceration and expand **court-sponsored** programming. Thus, this new method of release via third party custody became known as the **Intensive Pretrial Supervision Program.** For the most part, the individuals that qualified for this program were placed immediately into the custody of the D.C. Department of Corrections's halfway house. From there, case managers worked with the participants to establish compliance with program conditions. Moreover, random drug screening was a part of the requirements for program participants. In addition, the swift responses for program violations (i.e., positive urines) were attributed to the program's success. Reportedly, individuals that tested positive were immediately removed, and promptly remanded to custody at the D.C. Jail. In hindsight, both the strict narcotic supervision along with interactive program resources equally contributed to the accomplishment of program goals. Nevertheless, as the program was being brought on line, to the point of being fully operational, the players on the teams were at odds and misguided about its mission and eventually lost focus. The program resulted in a mixed bag of assets and liabilities. Unfortunately, more of the latter than former.

In addition, another program that was rapidly becoming the method of choice by pretrial services was called **electronic monitoring**. This new method being utilized by pretrial services was another tool implored to help stem the tide of an adherent crime wave in the metropolitan area. Now, at that time, electronic monitoring was the latest item on the market that required the use of an electronic bracelet.

And with new technology today due to the onset of computers the equipment is more sophisticated than what was used some twenty years ago. Today, they have tamper resistant bracelets, GPS Tracking devices, cell phones, scores of new approved databases to check and verify the exchange of Intel within the down side of an hour instead of waiting days for verification to be made. It is significant to note that today's technology is currently being designed to format the field of pretrial services will serve the community well. In fact, a telephone system that was modified to be interactive and formatted for pretrial agencies was considered an automated telephone check-in system. It permits the staff to monitor offenders placed on house arrest or under court-ordered curfews. The telephone was designed with a relay device, which automatically place calls and receive calls. Furthermore, new technology is being made available to pretrial services through the use of cellular phones, mobile phones, laptop, computers, etc. And these are critical elements in the officer's ability to keep up with the everchanging demands of their roles in the community. In closing, there are many ways in which pretrial services have proven to be an asset to the courts. Research has suggested that court sponsored programs have been credited with the following:

<u>PRETRIAL AND THEIR ASSETS TO THE COURTS</u>

1. Facilitates the compliance with court ordered conditions of release.
2. Ensuring that the defendant address court appearances ordered by the judges.
3. Helping break the cycle of crime through a series of early intervention programs.
4. Relieves prison overcrowding by helping to free space for serious criminal misconduct.

5. Has served to protect the community and rehabilitate the lives of individuals which would have otherwise been needlessly destroyed.
6. Allows the defendant to maintain employment while awaiting court proceedings.
7. Provides the judges with viable options and/or alternatives to detention.

With all that being said, the efforts that were made toward reducing overcrowding in the prison were considered as well respected tools which would continue to improve the agency over time. Consequently, the Lorton Complex welcomed the new technology that benefited the welfare of their community and the safety of their citizens as well. Nevertheless, with time whining down, Washington, D.C, had been issued a federal mandate to close all its prisons at the Lorton Complex by December 31, 2001. This raised the stakes of the game higher when operating within less than a two-(2)-year time frame for closure, yet, having crucial milestones and challenges still remain. The District faced the challenge of limited bed space in the Feds because they had an unexpected overcrowding in their own system as well. There was also the issue of medical transfers that faced impediments when evaluating the pros and cons of establishing perimeters for locations and/ or time travel concerns. Another issue was having the feds address the security/custody designation profiles which became an issue when the District used their own instrument to assess profiles. Yet, the Feds processed their assessments via a different version of what was considered a similar instrument. Consequently, there still remained between both agencies intense dialogue concerning which document would override the other because each instrument yielded different results. Also, the National Capital Revitalization and Self-Government Act of 1997 required that 2,000 inmates be transferred to private contract facilities by the year 1999. Nevertheless, on some accounts the private prisons had not yet been built, so there was not enough space to house the D.C. inmates awaiting interim placement in the federal system. Given this Federal mandate, the District was faced with a host of other unexpected challenges that were associated with meeting their goal. If looking for impediments from within, the lack of staff through closure and attrition cost the city extra money in paid overtime to cover staff compliment, constant management positions reshuffled, the parole authority changing their standards for parole criteria whereas many inmates unfortunately could not make parole, the revocation hearing processes were stymied along with massive amounts of halfway house escapees being returned as well. Therefore, bar none, all stop gap measures should have been on deck for Washington, D.C. primarily when it came to dealing with massive overcrowding. This being only two years removed from their closure date being mandated by federal law, there should have been new maps drawn in the sand if this target could not have been pulled off within the confines of a reasonable timeframe. According to the powers to be, although this was a formidable task nothing less would be acceptable than compliance with the federal mandate. So the District continued with its' move forward with the task at hand.

In hindsight, given some of the efforts that were etched out of sand just fell too short. The plans previously stated were good efforts, but they turned out to be a roust that backed the District in a much worst quagmire with vast overcrowding and limited resources. From there, the District was left in a worst state of affairs than it was from before. In fact, the federal government under the National Capital Revitalization and Self-Government Improvement Act of 1997, created the Court Services and Offender Supervision Agency (CSOSA) to specifically relieve much of the pretrial state level responsibilities. For the most part, this agency would step in where pretrial services left off. This move seemed to be the first move in what appeared to be seemingly in the right direction. And it alleviated a tremendous burden off the District in terms of dealing with its own affairs as well as the return of approximately 2,000 inmates per year returning from the Federal Bureau of Prisons (FBOP). Therefore, it was implemented per a federal mandated order as of 2001. And it remains in operation today.

Well, let's get back to Jimmy's arrival to the **Occoquan Facility** when he gets his crew together for his drug game expeditions with highly versatile flavor at the Lorton Complex. His bold, eager method of salesmanship just branded his product as something you had to have even though you knew you were wrong for having it. This was being caught up partly in the addiction and the culture at the same time. Jimmy was charismatic, quite impressive, and facilitated all the marketing that featured the new merchandise and improved method for sales of the product. He formulated all of the expertise and aplomb that generated much of the success behind the operation. The drug market was very much the same as any market. It's all about supply and demand. So after we made sure that the eagle had landed, all we had to do was set up the swoop. Once we got the loot inside, we're almost, or halfway home free. Then, we would check the merchandise to make sure it was legit. And if it was good, the next move was to send it by for inspection. From there, it went to Smokie, our hobby chemist. After that, we waited for the green light to go. Then, we went straight through all of our schemes for being tried and true phases. But for some of the transactions, we would by past certain formalities depending on the clientele. In most cases, our genuine mode of operation went something like this: we went from planning, marketing, soliciting, and distributing. Essentially, the operation is only as good as the players in the game. So me and my crew, we were in it to win it. We always brought home mo money than the competitors 'cause we had a better team. For the most part, it's simple math. Yeah, there are problems here and there. And you will have causalities along the way 'cause it's a war. Make no mistake this ain't no game. As with any operation, there were several options or choices that would advance the goals of the business proposition. Again, given the project at hand, some features worked out much better than others. I remember back in the day, all we did was bring our stash down to Lorton. If I recalled correctly, every week there was a delivery down at Lorton. I was not even locked up at the time, but I was still true to the game. There were many of my soldiers that went to jail and did time for me just so I could keep hustling on the streets of Washington, D.C. So yeah, we got it done. I remember, the old highway coat slide. Although it was just one of many operations, it had tested, tried, and true. Now, pulling off this gig called for seasoned hustlers no rookies. Anyway, in order to execute a coat slide, first of all, you needed a coat or jacket. Also, you needed your girl and her kids and that made the whole process much easier. But like I said, if you were a seasoned hustler then you could still get it done. But the move is not complicated, just move in a crowd, that's your cover up the crowd. But remember, allow your girl to stand in front of you. Always be the person standing in line directly behind her. Keep talking to her the whole time, never even acknowledge the officer except with a nod. And most of the time, he already knows how to play the game. If he's not down with the scam, then he won't even nod. So at that point, you got to work the crowd (i.e., you on your own), but you can still get in there anyway. From there, have your girl be the first to go through the scan laser to get searched by the wand. She will reach back to hand you her coat before she goes through. Next, on cue, have the kids run like gangbangers straight through the line. With all the commotion, you make sure the coat is loaded. Then quickly hand her the coat before she loses sight of the kids. Next, it's your time to get searched with the wand, but all of your stash was loaded inside the coat that you passed on to your girl. Once inside, just go to the bathroom and pass it off to him. We just hit a home run baby. Man, back in the day, it was like taking cake from a baby. We made that Lorton drop at least two to three times a week. We kept it tight. In our crew, it's practiced with precession. And this throwback (i.e., old school) move had for years been a powerful asset to our operation. Again, there were other such methods that were utilized to execute the sale of the product at Lorton as well. Nevertheless, gaining access was never a major problem. Anyway, we had bigger fish to fry.

Now, Jimmy and his crew were well known on the compound. He had locked down about 65% of the hustlers' paradise. But that was not a reason to be lax. Whenever, you get too lax, the lesson learnt from this type of business teaches you that you must go hard. You gotta to keep it hard all the way in this type of business or you fall hard. Now, even though Jimmy Black and his gang of thieves got locked up together on the same heist, they were not housed together. The last word that Jimmy got was that Cecil Sutton was being held at maximum security while both Larmar Taylor and Marlow McCoy were housed at Central Facility. So Jimmy relied on his Lorton crew to handle much of his marketing and sales operations. Most of this Lorton crew was made-up of his homies from the streets of Southeast, Washington, D.C. Even though every day was like a jungle, somehow Jimmy and his crew managed to keep the madness in check. And the teamwork was just like the crew that they ran out of Southeast, Washington, D.C. **They made almost as much juice hustling down at Lorton as they did on the streets**. The crew was getting ready for a big shipment to arrive for the family day celebrations scheduled in a couple of months. But Jimmy had ordered a sample trial run of the merchandise to get an idea of just what to expect. So at work the very next day, Jimmy had a talk with his boss man, Bobby Jennings. First chance he got with Bobby off to himself in the small briefing room, he was bold and direct. "Hey, man, yow we need to talk off the record. I need you to give Yogi my digits man. I've been trying to buzz that nigger for two days. I have not had any luck yet. Let him know that it's urgent, man. I'm low on just about everything. Tell him I'm ready for that K2 shipment right now 'cause I got my peeps lined up. Tell him to call me, right away, all right, man." As he slowly turned toward Jimmy to nod his head, the phone at the desk rang. And before Bobby reached out for the phone, he quickly turned around to acknowledged Jimmy and the stated, "Man, I'll get right on that." After he answered the phone, the work squad had their assignments for the day. From there, they all headed out to load up the truck for their workday. So with Bobby in full fledge overdrive mode, Jimmy followed close behind as he trod with agility in flight to keep up with his stealth strides all the way through the loading process to completion. On the real side, Jimmy liked working with Bobby a lot. Not only that, he enjoyed getting away from the prison for a while to see the city streets, it made him feel close to home once again.

Finally, the next day, Yogi called Jimmy. But something else happens first. From the beginning, I mean at first, I was doing quite well for myself all day, until I ran into my crew on the north walk and he said, "Hey, man, JB, I heard your case manager, Ms. Carleen Williams, wants to see you in her office, and she gets real mad when she's got to go look for a client, man." So the first words that came out of my mouth was, "What client?" Anyway, man, I ain't got time to fool with no Ms. Carleen, okay, you feel me?" From there, I left the walk and went right on back to hustling, baby. Jimmy then thought to himself, this prison life is real hard right now. Anyway, I did recall one day last week, one of these officers wrote a call out pass to see the case manager, but when he gave it to me, I threw it away. They have this controlled movement at Occoquan too, but not as strict as the D.C. Jail. This Occoquan is just an antiquated, old rusty, big dingy, dirty stinking, horseshoe style warehouse. I called it a shoe 'cause warehouses are lined up in the shape of a horseshoe. On one handle bar of the shoe is Occoquan zone I and the other side of the handle bar is called Occoquan zone II. That arch in the middle is where the kitchen is located. And Occoquan zone III is located behind the kitchen. It's separate and apart from the rest of the population. It supposed to be a fake drug program for real. Well, I know 'cause I conduct 50% of my business over on zone III. Anyway, my whole dorm is too crowed. I mean overcrowded for real. There's about two to three feet of space between each man in the unit. If things get any worst, this place gonna blow up again. And this time no parts of it will be left standing. I truly believe that any individual must understand that your mind have to be strong to handle any parts of Lorton. The beds are all double bunked. They are usually stacked in about four (4) to six (6) rows, with about fifteen to twenty to a row. This joint right here looks like a cross between a Mad Max bunker and a Frankenstein laboratory. Most of the time we have about ninety-five to one hundred inmates in each pod, but if that D.C. Jail can't clear their count (they must ship), due to a court order mandate Campbell vs. McGruder, then Lorton will get more inmates. The lighting is poor all around, but especially poor toward the back. The bunk beds are iron steel reels and coil springs. Then, you have a flat rubber straw mattress covered by one sheet and a blanket on top. The bathrooms are opened bay style with one petition like stall for just two commodes. The shower heads are six total, with no privacy curtains. The walls are all brick and mortar and the floors are cement. And then when it rains, the ceiling leaks water in the middle of the pod. So the whole pod hates rainy days. For the most part, all day long, all you can really see are brick and mortar. And Lawd please hold the stench (i.e., cow manure, bad hygiene, bad farts) or the flies. But on most days, there's a hefty dose of them both. If you feel the urge to exercise, then you can go to the field to lift weights or run. That way you can see a couple of trees and some green grass. If you're lucky, a couple of birds might fly by. But then the rest of the day has no agenda. I often turn to my higher source of power for which I know there is a God. So often, I pray. Sometimes, I even make to the chapel. Yes, even I do pray. I handle my sanity 'cause I stay busy all day working or hustling. I don't have time for Jerry Springer and I'm no Roy Jones Jr., either. I just keep it moving.

The survival of the inmate's classification process remained intact in spite of the institution being ravaged by extreme overcrowding. The sheer thought of the numbers that were removed from mainstream society without the hope of another chance to salvage their freedom warrants contempt. However, given the outrage over the present conditions at the Lorton Complex which hyped everyone's sense of negativity, hence, driving one dangerously too close over the edge. As a result of massive warehousing (approximately 39-40% over capacity) the facility experienced many adverse conditions resulting in limited bed space, inept resources, poor food quality, off-brand products, low-grade canteen items, excessive drugs, and violent conditions. The vocational trades were virtually nonexistent, and the drug treatment programs were a sham. In an effort to address concerns for programming, the case management team got involved to make the issue priority one. So after meeting with **Mr. Baukworth,** Supervisor. Occoquan, Zone 1, concessions were made to come up with programs for the inmate(s) population that the facility lost due to budget cuts and make efforts to supplement them. There were several of us that volunteered to facilitate the programs that were cut due to programming being considered low priority in the agency. The program that I selected was a case management prerelease program. This was an effort to better prepare the inmate to return back to the community from whence he came, yet, avoid the many pitfalls that expedites his return to custody. **Ms. Brown** selected a lifers program for inmates serving a life sentence. Essentially, these were a group of men that would not be returning to the community unless their hopes were rallied in U.S. Federal Court of Appeals. Ultimately, their ideal goals were to secure a new trial in federal court, hence, gaining another chance at freedom someday. On the other hand, learning to accept a prison lifestyle under the conditions of a controlled setting would be warranted in many of their cases as well. In addition, we have from another fellow colleague, **Mr. Glenn,** who selected an alternative to violence project. He instructed a counseling program for inmates with violent charges and/or violent tendencies. Quite frankly, if the truth be told, this program could benefit over half of the Lorton inmate population. And last but not least, **Mr. Ashford,** Recreation Specialist, organized and facilitated numerous sports tournaments and games. He organized basketball, wrestling, weight lifting sporting events, etc. **These activities were a major contribution that relieved much tension and stress throughout the confines of a relatively young (25-34 years old), flamboyant, aggressively charged overcrowded prison population as well.** With that being said, we cannot assume that everyone falls within the same category. In fact, all inmates are not the same. There were some that sought out a way of an escape. Some chose to involve themselves in sport activities and/or highly charged competitive exercise programs. Others went on a quest to pursue their academic endeavors and took up computers classes or the completion of their General Education Development (GED). Some even sought transfers to transition into vocational training programs. Then, there were the faith base groups that practice their religion to help them maintain their livelihood. The Islamic faith maintained a strong following at Lorton, but the Christian faith had a strong following as well. The quest for the Christian faith base journey could not have been attained if not for the volunteer ministry of Mrs. Bernice Slaughter. There was still this most interesting move of God facilitated by his most gracious servant in the work of her ministry. She was introduced to the Occoquan Facility by a family friend and heard the cry of suffering from the inmate population which inspired her to lend a hand. She began with starting a choir, then the construction of a chapel, and last but not least, the incorporation of the love ministry . . . EVOL spelled backward. When she answered the call of ministry to build the inmates a chapel at the Occoquan Facility, the project forever changed many inmates in the process of its construction. Ms. Slaughter incorporated EVOL (Every Volunteer of Love) Ministry at the Occoquan Facility and helped establish and built the Occoquan choir and chapel in May 1985. Excavating the construction of the chapel at the Occoquan Facility resulted in a spiritual rebirth in the hearts and minds of inmates destined for hope in spite of thorns of despair. The profound chronology of all her efforts are outlined in a book entitled, "When Grown Men Cry," by J.N. Slaughter, Jr. But still the mindset of a criminal culture intrigued and captivated many others. Then, you had the gang bangers, drug dealers, robbers, thieves, hustlers, sexual predators, etc., that continued their criminal activities despite being in prison serving time. Again, this is evidenced by letter(s) written to Mrs. Slaughter by one of the inmates in the EVOL Ministry program. The letter reads as follows from the book, "When Grown Men Cry," p. 87.

Dear Mrs. Slaughter,

I pray when this letter reaches you, you will still be doing God's work. I also want you to know this may be the hardest letter I am going to write. In this letter, I will try to help you understand how I got here, and what my life has been like since I started to use drugs. My reason for using drugs is because I was young, foolish, and wanted to know what life was all about. After ten years of pain and living lower than most animals, I have come to understand my life doesn't have to be like it is at this point. I am sure this letter won't come close to what I want to say about how my life has been, or I also understand that my fears and pain can't be put on paper. Most important, I understand at this point in time in my life, if I don't get some real help, I know I'll die from drugs. My last three years (as you know) I was supposed to be getting some help, at the same time being off the street down Occoquan. The help that I am talking about is my drug problem. That's one of the biggest jokes I've been a part of. **Occoquan has just as many drugs as 14th and W Street! I really never had a chance. I am weak for dope and when I was sent down there, the court knew that fact. What I think maybe the court didn't know was that I would be going nowhere I could really have a chance to make it and stay clean. Occoquan is not the place for me or anyone with a drug problem.** At the same time, I want you to know I've been to two drug programs before I came to Occoquan (Second Genesis and Last Chance) both was in an area filled with dope. Maybe I need to get away from Washington. At the same time, I need you to help me get this message across to whomever, so I really can get some help. I need your love and understanding more than I ever will at this point and time in my life. Please try to understand. I will die without your help.

Keep praying for me,

Mr. Hate-my-Self

D.C. #220-00

In closing, there are numerous letter(s) in the book written by the inmates to Mrs. Slaughter about their problems and concerns that they often face given the state of affairs in their lives while serving time in the D.C. Department of Corrections. The journey continues forward as the work of the ministry (i.e., love is contagious) makes bold and profound progress touching the lives of many.

Aside from all that, targeting the overcrowding issues at the Lorton Complex could go a long way toward stemming the tide of brazen criminality, aggressive violent assaults and/or murders at the Lorton prisons. Through the 1990s, the local newspapers, radios, and nightly news routinely featured articles of violent assaults, and brutal murders at the Lorton Complex. Consequently, much of the Lorton Complex became the breeding ground for the likes of ongoing criminal activities (opportunistic crimes). Reportedly, the Washington, D.C., metropolitan area in the 1980-1990s was often referred to as the murder capital of the world. These were considered as perilous times for the Washington, D.C, metro area. The staffing compliment remained low, but, the overcrowding of the prison population became a paramount issue when resources and supplies failed to keep pace with demand. Hence, management finally began to sit up and take note, and pay attention to the plight of the inmates within the Occoquan Facility. Nevertheless, in efforts to establish my program's approval, I had to submit to the warden a memorandum through the chain-of-command requesting permission for approval of program instruction. This was required for each program that we established. In fact, after the ad hoc routine measures of administrative rancor, all programs were approved for instruction at the Occoquan Facility. Nevertheless, my first contention went with much regard for young black males being warehoused in a brutal and violent prison without the hope or dignity from anyone that showed that they cared about their future. In fact, that whole scenario appeared to be a targeted segment of the population that had been locked away without any ties to the mainstream society. So again, what does a child do when they are suddenly separated from their parents? They cry! Their cries are only the beginning. We must find out what level of nurturing will be required to make that child whole again! If not, we will remain at war from the enemy from within. And unfortunately there are casualties of war. Unless we first come to grips with the reality of this type of warfare, then we will never understand that there are no winners in the game. There are just players with an agenda being used by management to exploit an adjunct mission delegated by beleaguered diplomacy. It is significant to note that the precursor for the closure of the Lorton Complex triggered the whining down of other agencies as well. Some entities included the following: prisons at Lorton Complex, community services, halfway houses, pretrial services, court services, parole board analyst, cooperation counsel offices, union representatives, etc. In fact, the department itself was a multifaceted organization with layers of management that fashioned their own personnel agendas. Nevertheless, with regard to the programs facilitated by the staff at the Occoquan Facility, there was no personal agenda. Specifically, with regard to the Case Management Pre-Release Program, this program truly wanted the inmates to succeed. Consequently, provisions had to be made in order for the offender to be thoroughly equipped to combat the potential for renewed criminal conduct. The Case Management Pre-Release Program was designed to educate and inform the inmate population about the standards, and expectations that will accompany the conditions of parole. Also, this program provided the inmate population with community resources and/or volunteer programs and professional nonprofit organizations that would substantiate the formation of successful reintegration. In addition, the program would cover the requirements for a formidable parole plan. Furthermore, the case management's perspective could in fact offer viable solutions to critical issues regarding postrelease needs, while providing the offender who is not eligible for Community Correctional Centers the opportunity to gain access to community resources that provide services for post-release needs. It was the intent of this program initiative to serve in a duel capacity with departmental provisions employed through the Employment Techniques Awareness Program (ETAP), which due to budget cuts operated within the parameters of what could be defined as limited capacity. So, the efforts put forth by the case management team were successful and receptive toward the inmate's treatment needs. This was a major milestone that set the stage for other programs to follow. In fact, upon approval on July 8, 1996, the Pre-Release program immediately set up shop for operation. At that point, I posted flyers throughout the facility announcing the Case Management Pre-Release Program and what it offered. I started with an introduction to the program curriculum and the signing of a contract. In fact, the curriculum established the program criteria for referrals. And the criteria were listed as follows:

1. Sentenced persons only.
2. Must be within six to eighteen months of Parole Eligibility Date (PED).
3. No disciplinary reports nor positive urines within the last year.
4. Must have completed the "Mandatory Adult Basic Education" requirements D.O. 4110.7.
5. Must be in compliance with both classification committee and parole board requirements.
6. Must have demonstrated the need for community program assistance.
7. Please be advised that class size will be approximately fifteen to twenty inmates.

8. Inmates must attend program orientation in order to examine and/or sign the program contract.
9. Please be advised all scheduling conflicts must be worked out in advance of program placement.
10. The Case Management Pre-Release Program would not be a substitute for "Life Skills."

This program from the start became one of the most popular programs on the compound. On the other hand, it was a lot of hard work. There was no magic wand to wave, just plain old hard work. In terms of case management services, the extra work kept me doing double time. But I was so impressed with the inmate's well-mannered behavior and their zeal for the program that it was well worth my efforts. So despite of the hard work and the litany of demands from the case management team, my reward in the end was simply to see them succeed. I considered the program truly a blessing from God, in that, as much as I thought I was teaching them, I found out at some point that there were also new things that were being taught to me. From there, I was much better prepared to excel in my newfound duties and responsibilities. The program itself was well received by the inmate population. As was more popularity and esteem, we received prominent guest invited from the community, scheduled videos (current affairs), demonstrated role plays (i.e., job hunts), performed skits, conducted mocked job interviews, completed job applications, résumés, job search letters, completed one year and five year plans, comprehensive class assignments, graduation ceremony (i.e., awarded letters/certificates of completion, etc.) In hindsight, this was a good program to get the inmate prepared to return to the community from whence he came. So upon completion of the application process, the inmates were screened to determine eligibility. After being accepted into the program, the inmates were instructed to attend an orientation to sign a contract. The contract process consisted of the requirements for program participation which were as follows:

DC DEPARTMENT OF CORRECTIONS
CASE MANAGEMENT SERVICES PRE-RELEASE PROGRAM
INMATE CONTRACT:

1. I _____ understand that attendance is mandatory.
2. I _____ understand that assignments must be completed and requires compliance with deadlines. Also, failure to complete classroom assignments is grounds for immediate termination.
3. I _____ understand that my attitude must be respectable and cordial to both staff and inmate population as well. Classroom decorum will be fully enforced and disruptions will not be tolerated.

I, also understand and will comply with the following pertaining to the above program:

a. Institutional dress code must be adhered to at all times.
b. Absolutely no phones calls will be permitted by the inmate population. All calls must be handled by your assigned dormitory case manager.
c. I must complete all eight program modules before a letter of appreciation is awarded.
d. The requirements for completing this program included the following items: parole plan, résumé, letter of correspondence, class assignments, and community resource referrals.

_____   _____
          INMATE   DATE

Finally, some of the assignments that the inmates would be required to complete included but were not limited to the following:

Program Syllabus: Case Management Pre-Release Counseling

WEEK#1—INTRODUCTION: An overview of the requirements for program completion explained with a review of program contract (see above), a briefing on assignment completion, required attendance, and suggested program research are thoroughly reviewed.

WEEK#2—GOAL SETTING: The program requires the formation of a one year and a five-(5)-year plan with specific step by step instructions including strategies for success. Reviewing the dynamics of conceptualization to motivate the mind set of success. Identify your assets relative to your strengths and skills, and conversely, identify your personal weaknesses to overcome your shortcomings. Developing an action plan and managing your plan (i.e, video). In addition, devising alternatives to include revisions for a backup plan.

WEEK#3—JOB SEARCH TECHNIQUES: Exploring the principles of work ethics. Realities of the job market, job application process, résumé & assessments, interviewing techniques, networking, principles of job search techniques. Researching community resources/referrals that compliment specific postrelease needs (guest speaker).

WEEK#4—THE DYNAMICS OF COMMUNITY TRANSITION: The most critical aspect of community transition is the jump from prison structure to the free world structure. Consequently every aspect of one's lifestyle will undergo alterations. Areas of concentration: Developing a positive attitude toward self and authority, Conflict Resolution, Interpersonal Skills, Stress Management, Family Survival Techniques, Coping Skills, Decision-Making and Drug Addiction. (Video)

WEEK#5—CLASSIFICATION AND PAROLE: In preparation for successful reintegration, the inmate's institutional conduct and program participation should be consistent with that of the parole board's requirement. There are five stages of incarceration, and each stage has a specific agenda designed to guide the inmate systematically through the prison system. The five stages of incarceration consist of the following: System Intake/ Initial Classification, Adult Diagnostic Study, Program Assessments/ Program Reviews, Preliminary Release Preparation, Post-Release Dynamics/ Community Programming. At this juncture, the office of Case Management Services facilitated the instructions to address concerns regarding the overall dynamics of the discharge process.

WEEK #6—JOB INTERVIEW PREPARATIONS/ REVIEW HIGHLIGHTS: Prepare for summation of program materials. Review program assignments, class projects, videos, quizzes, etc. Then, one of the final assignments is for each inmate assigned to complete UNIT #6 American Correctional Association (ACA) Pre-Employment Training curriculum and complete all worksheets. From there, the class is then divided into halves, with one-half being job seekers and the other half being employers. The class draws a card from a brown bag of assorted chips. Each chip contains a card with the assigned role to be played. Each player must assume his role and ultimately score enough points to get hired for the job. Upon completion: open discussion, comments, and feedback.

WEEK#7—DC PAROLE BOARD REQUIREMENTS: Follow up the summation for program and class completion: question and answers. Discuss requirements for parole supervision and the specific criteria that must be established prior to being released.

WEEK#8—GRADUATION: Ceremony conducted for presentation of certificates and appreciation letters.

The inmate(s) spent lots of time and energy volunteering as mentors that assisted others in the completion of class work materials in efforts to accomplish program goals. And the items that were awarded for all of their efforts were a **certificate and a letter of appreciation**. Although the certificate could not be listed the sample letter was included and reads as follows:

GOVERNMENT OF THE DISTRICT OF COLUMBIA
DEPARTMENT OF CORRECTIONS
OCCOQUAN FACILITY
BOX 85
LORTON, VIRGINIA 22199

DATE _____

MEMORANDUM

TO   :   INMATE _____

            :   DCDC# _____

FROM   :   CARLEEN WILLIAMS
                   CASE MANAGER, ZONE 1

SUBJECT :   LETTER OF APPRECIATION

REF   :   CASE   MANAGEMENT   PRE-RELEASE
                   COUNSELING PROGRAM

This letter of appreciation is being presented on behalf of inmate _____ DCDC# _____ for _____ participation in the Case Management Pre-Release Counseling Program at the Occoquan Facility. This program was designed to equip the inmate population with community resources and/ or services provided through the auspices of community volunteer programs and professional nonprofit organization that promulgates support services targeted for community transition.

Inmate _____ has been a participant in Case Management Pre-Release Counseling Program since _____. He has demonstrated a positive disposition with the willingness to research, explore and articulate the composition of resource materials for classroom demonstration.

The program required the completion of a one year and five year plan which includes specific personal and professional goals hoped to accomplish upon eventual release. Instructions were also presented for completing résumés, job applications, strategies for success, preparing for parole, techniques for successful interviews, setting realistic goals, time management, stress management, conflict resolution, self-esteem, strengthening family ties, and coping with negative peers.

For additional information regarding the contents of this letter and/or the subject for which the information was provided, please contact Ms. Carleen Williams, ext. 6619.

The overall operations of the Case Management Pre-Release Program continued to turn out program awards every eight weeks with graduation classes looking to make their mark in the world for some good. These milestones were badges of pride for our clients despite of the on sought of negativity. As indicated earlier, the Case Management Pre-Release Program was indeed a success. Nevertheless, in order for the program to succeed, I had to solicit the services of many community service volunteers, benevolent organizations, rehabilitative programs, religious organizations, etc. In addition, I would often contact numerous public and/or private therapeutic counseling programs in an effort to solicit specialized services for inmates with special needs. Furthermore, I solicited the services of staff members at the Occoquan Facility and convinced them to render their talents and expertise to service their communities by imparting accolades that empower the inmate population, and applauded their efforts to succeed. Consequently, given the hard work, persistence, and determination, the program did succeed. From there, I took it upon myself to facilitate the orientation for the program. I felt it was important to set the tone and the pace along with the expectation of the program goals. I instructed various class modules included in the eight week seminar as well. The program turned out to be one of the most popular seminars at Lorton. It remained at the Occoquan Facility for approximately eighteen months. In fact, the program itself remained in operation (. . . . well intact) until I was transferred to the Maximum Security Facility in April 1998.

NOW, LET'S GO BACK TO SOME OF CARLEEN'S ACTIVITIES AT THE WORKPLACE.

BUT FIRST THIS STAFF MEETING WITH **MR. BAUKWORTH, CHIEF CASE MANAGER, ZONE 1,** WAS ESSENTIALLY ABOUT A DIRECTIVE THAT CAME DOWN FROM GRIMEKE BUILDING, 1928 H STREET, NE WASHINGTON, D.C. THE DOC HEADQUARTERS THAT THE AGENCY START THE PROCEEDINGS TO FACILITATE THE TRANSFER OF 500 INMATES TO AN OUT-OF-STATE FACILITY IN OHIO. THESE

PACKAGES HAD TO BE COMPLETED WITHIN FIVE WORKING DAYES. THIS OF COURSE WOULD MEAN OVERTIME BEING PAID out to case management staff. WITH THAT BEING SAID, we would literally be jammed up against the wall. The meeting commenced with the arrival of our supervisor, **Mr. Baukworth.** "Good evening everybody, I just wanted to call this meeting, just to revisit some of the old issues that we left on the table from our last meeting. In addition, to update you on this new project that just came down the pipe. There is a new mandate to expedite the immediate transfer for 500 inmates to Youngstown, Ohio. I know you all are working hard in adverse conditions. We have accomplished so much to be proud of. Everything that the feds have thrown our way, we were able to accomplish. They still look at us and wonder how was it possible that we managed to perform so well with so little. Yet, they have refused to admit that our case management staff was equally comparable by any standard to their organization. But time and time again, we came through. Let the truth be made known that nothing can move out of D.O.C. without being facilitated by case management services. Lastly, I just want to say thank you. Thank you all. And again, you are greatly appreciated for all that you do. And remember that nothing can be transferred or shipped out without you. At this time, I would like to open the floor for comments or concerns at this point." Then, Ms. Brown had to make her sentiments known by all.

Now, as Yogi spoke to Jimmy, on his cell phone, he was in a smoked filled room of one of the trap houses out of southeast. "Hey, my niggar, what up?" Then a brief moment of slience . . . followed by, "Man, I need your services right away. I got the squad on the radar, so I know all the moves. Tell me you still holding my ticket. Yo man, you still got my ticket with all that I ordered for the next drop, it's still legit. Man, you can double that white horse. I can shadow the stash for pick up." At that point, Yogi was in the middle of a fast break with a heist, but he knew that Jimmy was a category VIP clientele and that his order was top priority, so he knew he had to get it done. So Yogi dropped his score and switched out with his running dog MEME. He returned his attention to Jimmy and repeated the order to clear the ticket for the run. From there, he promptly stated "Hey, Jimmy, let me run this ticket down so you can make sure we all good. Now, this here is what we got so far, the **blue ice, white diamonds, panama reds, Columbia gold, the Xanax (benzodiazepines) wonk, some hurricanes, some bebe's methamphetamines, K2 (synthetic cannabinoids), marijuana, ecstasy, and white horse (double)."** After listening to Yogi with the full run down, Jimmy sat back and smiled with a sense of feeling secure about the ground game of his operation, but he didn't want Yogi to feel too cocky so he didn't let he catch on. "Man, y'all got to stay with the game plan. Man, y'all tighten up out there, I can't reach y'all man." Yogi, listening intensely released his quick snap back, "Man, we here all day long man, check your digits man, check your digits." Jimmy is just laughing round about now, and after a long pause, he finally says, "Yow, man, that ticket right there is good." Yogi, then slowly replies, "I know you straight, man, if nobody else is straight round this Mama Jama, you straight, man, ok. I got you man, I got you." And I got the drop too. Now, at that point, Jimmy is quite impressed, yet he still manages to contain himself. "So, man, Yogi, I'm out of here! Later, man, I'll meet you at the drop." Yogi, takes that as a good move, and then slowly replies, "Later, JB."

CARLEEN, continues her work at the prison while overseeing the Case Management Pre-Release program as well. In fact, all of the programs are running quite well, yet, the overcrowding remains prevalent among the INMATE population. There were many changes that took place within the case management staff and throughout the agency as well. We had lost several staff members as a result of the eminent mandate for closure. We had lost at least four case managers and two supervisors from Occoquan. And right away, we made it known that we needed more staff to replace them or we could never get caught up to speed. Furthermore, the inmate population could not be serviced nor could the programs continue their operation. There were also lawsuits throughout the Lorton Complex causing many mid/high-level managers to get shuffled around. At Occoquan alone, we literally saw five different wardens get assigned and subsequently get reassigned, or lose their lawsuits and get fired. In fact, on one occasion, the Deputy Executive Director resigned or stepped down due to a warrant being issued for his arrest, allegedly due to late child support payment to the state of Texas in June 1998. Furthermore, he was allegedly being investigated for approving 1,000+ hours of overtime for his office assistant that he reportedly could not justify. So these were troubling times in the agency. Also, after many of the halfway houses closed, their staffs were re-assigned to Lorton, And Occoquan retained much of their staff. We were happy to get the help, but we quickly came to grips with the fact that halfway houses do not operate like prisons. Therefore, in some cases, staffs were receptive toward the prison culture and operations and others were not. So it was a hard struggle to get halfway house staff to adapt to a new way of life behind the wall as opposed to being hamstrung by their community services playbook. Nevertheless, the journey continues. The overcrowding conditions at the prison system at Lorton still created a stressful workplace environment which wreaked havoc on the staff compliment and the limited resources being dispensed. In addition, there continued to be a substance abuse problem at the prisons at Lorton. When inmates were being assaulted daily for bad drug deals, gang bangers hustling, money laundering, soliciting sexual activities, and staff commandeering all facets of the operation to get paid, the warden held it all down. Even the test results from the urine samples were alarming. According to the results from the urine test, 40% of the overall population tested positive for marijuana, cocaine, or PCP. The warden knew that he had a major problem, but he didn't know how to turn it around. All of those drugs could not have just come from road squad. Now, some of those drugs must have come right in through that front gate. There were lots of dirty staff being caught up for bringing in drugs to these inmates. Meanwhile, the letters were still being circulated throughout Lorton. The letters "DID YOU KNOW" remained the highlight of Lorton's gossip to date. Anyway, staffs' tension grew more strained due to anticipated lawsuits. And this coupled with the staff anxiously awaiting the Reduction-in-Force (RIF) list to come down, all of Lorton was on edge. Almost every week, there was an agency that was due to close down and staffs were to be immediately reassigned if space were available. Aside from that, staffs were lost when it came to trying to figure out if they were next to be RIF or not. So of course people were scrambling to get a letter "DID YOU KNOW," just to find out about the RIF list or at least the latest gossip.

Meanwhile, the new staff along with case managers at Occoquan Facility continued their assignments. The mayor has just last week signed another executive order for Emergency Powers Act (EPA) to relieve overcrowding at Lorton. So this mandate for case management services meant overtime pay and extra hours at work until all cases were processed. This assignment came on the heels of processing five hundred (500) inmates for Red Onion, Virginia, the week before last. The way the inmates kept shipping out of Lorton they were well on their way to trying to get this whole damn place closed. But guess what? These fools kept getting locked up, over and over again.

Anyway, Carleen was in the process of reviewing her caseload when she discovered the name of one inmate that she never interviewed. For some reason, his name looked familiar, but his face just didn't click. She knew that he hadn't been interviewed 'cause she had no emergency contact information available on him. Now, she knew, she had to see him ASAP.

Finally, Jimmy Black Blango gets to meet Ms. Carleen: "Good afternoon Mr. Black, my name is Ms. Carleen Williams, and I am your case manager. Have a seat, and by the way, first, I would like to cover a few

documents. I need to complete this mental status exam, review your intake profile and get an emergency contact. From there, I will schedule you on the docket for classification. From there, the agenda containing the overall format for the inmate interview would proceed in the manner that followed a series of questions similar to the ones cited below:

Now, let me begin by asking you for your full name? Address and phone number?

What is your mother's name? Address and phone number?

What is your father's name? Address and phone number?

What is your marital status? Single, Married, or Divorced?

What is your spouse's name, address, phone number?

Do you have children? If so, how many and list their names and dates of birth?

What is your current address?

Who do you list as an emergency contact? List primary and secondary.

List both parties' name, address, phone numbers?

What have you experienced during this term of incarceration that would alter or impact your concept of criminal activity?

Where did you stand with future plans and goals prior to incarceration? And vice versa where do your plans and goals stand now?

From there, I can take over and prepare all of the other documents for you to complete. So just a moment please. Thank you.

Once again, the intake orientation process is conducted by the office of case management services. It is a thorough investigative process that takes about forty-five to fifty minutes. It requires screening volumes of background data which is then utilized to designate housing requirements, formulates program assessments, and recommend treatment referrals. As previously stated, the case manager collects scores of background data, personal data, family history, emergency contacts, and medical history. The interview will also include a mental status exam. Essentially, a series of questions and observations along with medical history which then helps gage the inmates' preliminary score(s) for suicidal tendencies and/or emotional instability. In addition, it is required that the case manager review the inmates' protective custody status, escape history, court ordered separations, special handling requirements, academic background, vocational skills, or training, employment history, substance abuse history, criminal profiles, or crimes of choice. From there, the inmate is issued an orientation booklet and/or a copy of the Lorton Regulations Approval Act of 1982. For the record, this piece of legislation outlines inmate behavior that violates departmental policy. The booklet contains a list of all the charges of misconduct for which an inmate can receive a disciplinary report. Upon completion, the case manager will schedule the inmate for classification. At the meeting for classification, the case manager will present an overview of the inmates' materials before a committee of members along with the inmate. After reviewing all the data presented, recommendations for programs, custody reviews, and treatment referrals for the inmates are made. These members include colleagues from our treatment teams. They are academic/vocational teachers, program counselors, staff at the medical/mental health services, psychological services administrative personnel, chaplain services, and security personnel.

MS. KELLY: "SHE'S A SHARP, PIGEON TOED, HARD NOSE PENCIL PUSHING DWEEB, for all intense and purposes." But these meetings held for staff whenever Ms. Kelly called them were nothing but gossip sessions. Now, Ms. Brown didn't disappoint at all. And she was just dying to take the floor. Now, in this particular meeting, almost everyone was there except Mr. Baukworth, who didn't like the hint of gossip to entertain any part of his conversations. So without further delay, Ms. Brown took the floor. "Well, Ms. Kelly as you well know that we are concerned about the final status of the RIF and just where we stood on the list. We had already gotten word from Grimke Building, DOC headquarters, that approximately fifteen case managers will be losing their jobs on this round of RIFs. Now, recently the union reps alerted staff to this new program placement for displaced workers. This new priority placement program set up for us by the Feds was set-up to benefit only a select few. And their selection process remains unknown to date, no pun intended. And we haven't heard anything else from the union reps either. We have not seen another letter, "DID YOU KNOW." The actual closure of our facility here at Occoquan is coming at the end of this fiscal year (reportedly 1999). And I know that much to be true because some of us have already received letters of reassignments. There are volumes of lawsuits throughout the department. The D.C. Jail were racked with them. There are cases of lieutenants whom are married, yet, they have been caught allegedly sleeping with their own sisters-in-law, given the fact that they both worked at the same facility. Also, there are cases that allegedly got the warden at the Central Detention Facility caught up in lawsuits because she ended up having an affair(s) with her employees. She had allegedly got caught with several other staff members at one time. Hence, lawsuits filed. Not only that, the inmates allegedly bought lawsuits against her too. Well, there is no end to the lawsuits in sight. One lieutenant was married and allegedly carried on an affair with a case manager, yet, refused to leave the wife and kept the case manager as well. He paid her rent, her car notes, bought her clothes, food, and everything. Reportedly, he still does to this day. And you cannot tell me that her name does not appear on the RIF list. Now, tell me why not? And you know everybody knows about the captain that took the officer's wife (administrative secretary) and played his deck of cards from the top of the deck 'cause he simply didn't care who knew he took her from her husband. The officer worked for him on his same shift and they still refused to move the officer to another shift. Man, that was such a sad situation. So this Lorton mess can get to be real nasty, you know what I mean? These lawsuits are seeping through the gallows of every guard post at the Lorton Complex. Somebody needs to look into these concerns and address this urgent matter. And if not, what happens when all of our careers are compromised, and our reputations are inadvertently tainted in the shadows of vicious ongoing court litigations (i.e., lawsuits)? Unfortunately, there appears to be no end in sight.

Jimmy, has now returned from his job on the work squad:

Now, JB was anxious and on edge because he was looking for that last word from Yogi to confirm that drop for the swoop. So he decided to stay calm and just wait it out. He thought to himself how that today was Sunday and that he had to get word by 6:00 a.m. Monday morning or all bets were off. But he still had lots of time before time ran out to get word from Yogi. All he needed to do was to simply chill 'cause time and time again, Yogi always came through and he would come through again.

Meanwhile, he told himself to chill. At that point, he thought of his best friends, his homeboys, his old crew. He wondered about Cecil Sutton, Larmar Taylor and Marlow McCoy. These had to be the best friends anybody could have. Man, we all grew up together. We went to elementary school, junior high, and high school together. We got expelled together, severed time together, and gang banged together. Man, I miss all those guys. But I'm fine right here where I am right now. I can get almost anything I want. I can get cigarettes, marijuana, coke, and I eat well. It's just bad 'cause I don't have my freedom. I don't want to see my daughter down here to this prison. I told all my family to stay away from here 'cause I'm fine. I just don't want their contact until I'm free. That's just what I feel. Man, I'm deeply passionate about that man, God knows I am. Man, I got here by myself and I got to serve this time by myself . . . BEEP, BEEP, BEEP, BEEP, BEEP, BEEP, BEEP, BEEP, BEEP, BEEP, BEEP, BEEP, BEEP JIMMY PULLS OUT HIS PHONE. HE MUZZLED THE PHONE TO SILENCE THE NOISE. HE ALMOST FORGOT TO BE DISCRETE 'CAUSE NIGGARS BE TRIPPING OVER THE PHONE MAN. ANYWAY,

WITH RAZOR SHARP EYES CAUGHT AND LASER LOCKED ON THE RED FLASHING DOT ON THE MESSAGE ICON, HE THEN PRESSED THE MUTE BUTTON TO BLOCK NOISE MADE BY THE PHONE. FROM THERE, HE QUICKLY PRESSED THE MESSAGE BUTTON. THEN, THE TEXT WAS REVEALED.

"HEY, JB, GOT THE DROP READY FOR THE SWOOP."

"PICKUP READY MONDAY AT 1100 HOURS, CORNER OF 14th STREET & H STREET S.E., WASHINGTON, D.C."

"IT'S ALL GOOD JB, AND, JUST LIKE ALWAYS YOU KNOW THE EAGLE HAS THE SWOOP."

"LATER, JB!"

After Jimmy read the text, he immediately strolled to his contacts and pressed Yogi. When his info popped up on the screen, he then pressed message and started a quick TEXT MESSAGE back to Yogi.

"HEY, YOGI, GOT THE TEXT, AND ALL EAGLES CAN FLY!"

"JUST RUN IT LIKE LAST TIME AND WE GOOD!"

"I GOT THE SWOOP?"

"LATER, YOGI!"

From there, Jimmy was ecstatic about the closing of the deal. So he planned to go to bed early and get up early in order to get ready for work at sunrise. In fact, Jimmy was in such a good mood that he even allowed several inmates to use his phone for family leisure calls. He permitted free calls on his phone for 'bout two to three hours all the way up till his bedtime. Then, he went on to his bunk. He laid down and went to sleep. And he was up early the next morning at sunrise. Jimmy knew he would have a busy day. But he was ready to go to work on time. And after he made his way out of the dorm over to the workshop, he was beaming full alert and jacked up on caffeine (3 cups of coffee). But his boss man, **Bobby Jennings**, was already there waiting for the inmate(s) and the rest of his squad. Now, Jimmy got a minute off the record with **Bobby Jennings** to let him know about the swoop. And the boss man understood, and agreed to make the swoop on time. So when the rest of the squad arrived, they got the equipment, loaded the truck, and took off for work. In fact, today the squad had to make stops at three different work sites. And that was just find by Jimmy 'cause he knew boss man would make the swoop on time. So Jimmy sat quietly and continued to collect his thoughts for the business of the day. He thought to himself, man, nobody understood the gang bangers like the gang bangers themselves. The gangs are as vociferous as human nature would allow, yet, as carnivorous as one's instinct could project. The whole D.C. culture was more than a way of life for gang bangers it was all that they lived for. It was the only institution that they felt that they controlled for themselves. The gangbangers have always felt under seize and this type of mindset has always been a part of their indoctrination. Now, whether this is a conspiracy theory that's real or imagined, it's the philosophy that bonds their groups together. The gangs were where they drew the last line, it was the last frontier. Their true belief was that blacks have always been under some form of oppression since the beginning of time. Yet, they survived throughout the generations with the same principles built on many of the groups that faced oppression as well. For the most part, mankind tends to be a gregarious creature within his own rights. Nevertheless, it is the very same concept within the black community as a whole. Throughout many aspect of society, the black communities are herded like cattle while being lulled to sleep and blinded by the inertia of oppression. Yet, they are not aware of their second-class citizenship. My stomach became bitter as gall as it bubbled over and drowned in the toxic fumes of indignation. So Jimmy felt that this gang life was worth taking a look at, for all its worth. If it could mobilize our cause to get equal share of the monopoly franchise and lift our people up, then the gang might not be so bad. Jimmy felt that if gang banging could cause some good in the world than why not give them a try? And just like that, with the blink of an eye, his mind switched back to the reality of his long bumpy truck ride in the back seat of the inmate county work squad truck, amongst seven other inmates, liberated by seeing the city lights. Now, the truck kept rolling slowly down the highway as their destination began to appear on scene. They were now approximately two blocks from the target for pick-up. As Bobby approached the stop light at the intersection and waited for the light to turn green, Jimmy knew that his crew had already laid the trap. So all he had to do was located the brick and make the swoop. Just as the light turned green, his eyes locked on the target through the window of the moving truck. And before Bobby rolled straight through the traffic light, Jimmy had already spotted the building with the marker for the brick. He saw it just prior to the truck making its turn into the parking lot. At that point, it was approximately 10:58 a.m., about two minutes prior to the swoop. From there, Jimmy began to calculate his next move to get the hammer on the swoop and load it on the truck for transfer. So Jimmy just sat quietly until the time came for them to exit the truck, and then he could make his move. Shortly after the truck was parked, Bobby made all remain seated until they were briefed on their assignment for the day. Upon his completion of the itinerary, along with a brief question and answer session, Bobby then permitted them all to exit. Once I got off the truck, I knew my next move. And sure enough my crew had laid that trap. I waited until the whole squad was inside the building being occupied with moving heavy debris. Then, I shimmed over to the brick wall marked with the letter X. I kneeled down on one knee at the spot located below the X. Then, with a brisk stiff jab of the right heel of my shoe, the box top surfaced through the gravel. Bobby knew the plan was to keep his squad busy until I rejoined the group back inside the building for duty. So after I got the box loaded and secured back on the truck for transfer, I was home free. After I made that move, I rejoined the group. From there, Bobby knew I was ready for transport.

Now, it was all up to Bobby to work his magic. And work it, he did. As the truck pulled up alongside the gate's entrance to Occoquan, Bobby put on his game face and popped his collar. At that point, he put his foot down on the pedal to shift the gear into park. Then, he sat behind the wheel of the truck, chin up, stiff neck, and stern as the officer approached the vehicle. "Hey buddy, what's up? How's it going?" Bobby leaned back in his seat, and slowly replied, "Hell, man it's all good, I'm just trying to flip this bird right now! Look man, I got to make a quick move right now, just get me in the yard and out of this sally so I can get on my way." The officer replied, "Well, when you got to go you gotta to go." And from there, he abruptly returned to the booth and quickly went inside to flip the switch allowing the truck to pass through the sally. At that point, Bobby put his foot back down on the pedal, shifted the gear to drive causing the truck to skeet forward. Amazingly, we cleared the checkpoint within the down side of two minutes. From there, we were on our way. Then, once inside, we unloaded the truck. We got all the equipment off the truck and put it away. And just before it was time to leave work for the day, the inmates made their usual brief chats with Bobby and then said their goodbyes and they left. Now, with just Bobby and I left alone, it was time to survey the merchandise. So I went straight to the door of the backseat of the truck and pulled out the bricks. "Man, wow, that Yogi really did knock that job out, he got it all straight. So man, for now, we were locked and loaded." And even Bobby, slowly nodded his head with a big wide smile, signifying his approval." So first things first, you know I got to call, Smokie to get the 411. But let's just table that for now 'cause we got mad cash on the line, and it's all fresh bait, man, just like always." But Jimmy hated to cut corners and he usually never tried to ditch the protocol, 'cause he didn't see the urgent need. Then, Jimmy jumped in Bobby's face to square off. He stood an inch away from his left ear, with a brass deep baritone voice barking loudly, "Man these guys ain't going nowhere. We've got what's called a captive audience, they ain't going nowhere. They're just junkies and they can wait for the first twenty-four anyway, man, that's just procedure, you know that, Bobby. Now, if they want to do business elsewhere, than let them be. It's just that simple."

Bobby jerked abruptly away from what he felt like was a blast in his left ear. To some degree, he lost his bearings within the mix of emotions, not to mention being caught off guard while being played like a sucker or perhaps being dissed (disrespected). He then put some distance between them both. At that point, he was in a defensive stance. But then with a less combative tone being detected from JB, he was able to regain his composure. From there, he finally agreed with Jimmy to stick with protocol. At that point, the show was back on the road, and now the next move would be to give Smokie a shot at the first twenty-four. And then move on from there. Shortly after that, Bobby said, "Okay, man, you got it, you right, man. I just wanted to come clean on a deal. I previously set up a big deal that I needed to closeout right away. But for real man, I can just wait for the first twenty-four."

From there, both men secured their bricks for the following business day. They were adamant about their agreement on the deal for Smokie to clear the first twenty-four. Although that was what Bobby agreed to with Jimmy, he had a whole different scenario in mind which was to finish what he had started on yesterday. He had made up his mind to get his stash from the bricks no matter what Jimmy said. And Bobby waited until he could verify that Jimmy was gone, and that all work squads were cleared from the unit, before he made his move. Now, Jimmy headed back to his block to wait out the first twenty four just like he and Bobby had agreed on. So wait it out, he did.

Bobby returned to the stash hidden at the workstation and recovered the merchandise. He moved quickly before anyone could see him enter inside or exit and leave out. Once the workstation had been cleaned of all scatted debris, he secured the area, locked up the shop and went on his way.

TAHOE BLANGO: Tahoe struggled alone to keep her kids and a roof over their head. At this point, Tahoe is still at home busy raising the kids. They were growing up fast now. Jimmy has been locked up now for almost three years and the time has gone by so fast. Tahoe has missed him dearly. She hopes that he makes it home during the early part of next year. So, provided that God have mercy and grant her prayer for JB to come home, it will be a special time in her life. She understood his position on his stance about visiting so she never pushed the issue that much. Anyway, on previous occasions when Tahoe visited it caused her medical concerns. In fact, she remembers visiting him when he first got locked up approximately two years ago, and that same night when she got home, she could not sleep. And, from there, a series of nightmares, which prompted episodes of anxiety attacks. These visits triggered a whole lot of mental anguish, undue stress, and hardship that Tahoe could not bear with the added responsibilities of raising a family on her own. So, a year ago, she decided to reframe from putting herself through that ordeal and resorted to writing JB letters or just waiting for his phone calls. And that's what JB and his family agreed upon. Now, JB loved his mom and for him that was exactly the way he wanted it to be. He would always say, "I got myself in this jail by myself, so I am going to have to serve this time by myself." This was how JB wanted to serve his time. He knew his family was there for him. He knew that they all love him. He just never felt that putting through any parts of the prison experience was dignified. He felt like by him being a man that it was his responsibility to spare them from trauma shock. Even his small child, he refused to have her be inoculated by the ravages of (the house of ill repute) an ill-reputed indigenous prison lifestyle. Nevertheless, Tahoe had many other responsibilities herself as being the primary caretaker in her own household. At this point, Tahoe had five children altogether including JB. The oldest at home with her now was a beautiful brown girl, just like her mom, named Jasmaine Marie Blango, nineteen years old. Then, there was another pretty girl named Lashay Marie Blango, fourteen years old. Next, was a handsome young man named Kevin Montel Blango, nine years old, and last but not least was another good looking charismatic young man named Marcus Lea Blango, seven years old. These kids were all that Tahoe lived for. They were her life, her heart and soul. And she prayed to God every day that her son, JB would return home soon, to rejoin the family so that they could all enjoy the blessings of God together. So, Tahoe knew firsthand what it was like to be abandon, casted away and alone. After all, this was her legacy at the tender age of eighteen years old, when she was kicked out of her house by her own mom, when she found out about her pregnancy. She has never tried to return back home in Louisiana, nor has she ever looked back. The whole experience was too painful for Tahoe to bear the thought of, so she usually just blocks it out. And over the years, the practice of erasing the memory of her past served her quite well. She just learned how to delete certain experiences from her past and move on. She had moved on with her life. Although her relationships with men never lasted very long, she remained optimistic about her future to perhaps marry someday. The only man that ever spent any extensive time with her was JB's dad. But that chapter in her life was short lived as well. She would always say when faced with difficult times, and she had faced many that, "With God all, things are possible." And that was what Tahoe truly believed as well. Today, Tahoe was a thirty-nine-year old single, Afro-American female raising her family in the District of Columbia. Tahoe lived in a four bedroom condominium in Barry Farms, Southeast, Washington, D.C. where she has resided since JB was a small child. She has raised all here children there as well. Her kids attended D.C. public schools. She received public assistance from the D.C. Department of Social Services and lived in D.C. low-income housing projects as well. Tahoe was truly thankful to God for all his blessings to her and her family. And she gives God all the credit for where she is and how far he has brought her because without the love of God, she knew she would not be here today. Now, Tahoe never got the opportunity to get her high school diploma, so last year, she went to night school and was able to complete the classes for her General Educational Development (GED). From there, she wants to pursue a degree in Early Childhood Education. Therefore, she applied for grants and loan programs at the University of the District of Columbia, where she awaits final approval. So her kids are very proud of her. Meanwhile, Tahoe works at a cleaning detail service for cars at **Moe's Car Wash.** And her daughter, Jasmaine works at Burger King. The whole household has busy schedules. So both Tahoe and Jasmaine take turns with the family routines for the kids. Whenever Tahoe is at work, Jasmaine stayed home with the kids. And vice versa, whenever Jasmaine worked, Tahoe stayed at home. That way the kids had discipline, structure, and were well supervised. And with all that going for her, she thanked God for her lucky stars. So one day at work, Tahoe noticed that the traffic all day was heavy. She had worked all day nonstop without a break. So as the last car approached the platform, she thought to herself, this is my last one, I never got a break. Then she promptly let Moe know that this was her last customer, and that she would wrap up her shift when she finished. Upon completion, she intended to clock out and go home. So with the actual thought of leaving for the day, a spark of fire weld up inside. Now, with a boost of energy to spare, she turned around with an extra bounce in her step. And like a fine-tuned robot, she begin restocking her supplies. She made sure that she had new cleaning solutions, brushes, clothes, gloves, etc. From there, she was ready. Now, as Tahoe approached the platform, she had everything she needed to make the car look like a showcase classic. This gentleman who was the owner of this car was very peculiar. He said his name was Yogi, and that he owned a landscaping business in the District. He handed me a card and told me to call if I needed his services and that first time callers received automatic 15% discounts. Nevertheless, all I could think about were the kids and how fast could I get home? By the way, I do remember slipping the card into my coat pocket before starting the cleaning job. As I got started, I noticed that almost every section of his car (Cadillac 1998) was nearly in the original pristine factory model condition. This car was a pleasure to detail, 'cause it didn't seem like you were cleaning it at all. It seemed more like a model for a showcase. Anyway, as I got into the front seat, the armrest had a picture posted inside. **I just couldn't help but stare. I was shocked. There was a picture of Yogi and a guy that I knew had to be Black. And, not just any Black, but my baby's daddy Black. JB's father was the guy in that picture. I was frozen in time. My mind flipped backward, forward and did several cartwheels.** The sound of Moe pressing the wash pedals in the cleaning booth startled me. Shortly after that, I was instantly released from the trance and brought me back to my reality. Nevertheless, I was completely embarrassed by the last round of events, and hoped that no one had discovered anything about my private moment. Anyway, I finished the job quickly in hopes to inquire more information from Yogi about that picture. So I quickly closed out the detail job and wrapped up all the paperwork for him to sign. I made small talk about how clean he kept the car. He said thanks and welcomed the remarks. So I went a step further and asked how long he had it? Where he bought if from? Was he interested in selling it? He just smiled the whole time, but never answered any questions. Then, I inquired about the picture. He appeared somewhat confused, but, answered anyway. He said that the guy in the picture was his uncle, Cadillac Black. I was speechless. I played it off. Then, he reached into his wallet and pulled out a crisp new $100.00 dollar bill to pay for the services. I quickly took the cash, handed him his car keys, and give him a receipt. He appeared to be quite pleased and smiled as walked away. From there, he got inside the car and drove away. When I finally got home, I was no more good. I told Jasmaine everything. She was excited about the possibility of Jimmy being able to finally meet his dad. Jasmaine said it was a sign. She said that God's angels were protecting Jimmy. So Jasmaine said that it was good news. I was just baffled. I told Jasmaine that my next move would be to write Jimmy a letter and explain everything. So that's exactly what I did.

Mr. Baukworth has called for another staff meeting to discuss a project for case management services once again. He starts by citing to staff how proud he is of all of us for accomplishing so much given limited time frames. Yet, he immediately lays out the task at hand. "So you see the mayor office has invoked another round of emergency provisions for the Emergency Powers Act (EPA), to go into effect ASAP. This means that all current task at hand has to be tabled or put away due to executive order by the mayor. So this really takes our staff for a loop every time it's invoked because that means that all cases scheduled for classification must be put on hold. From there, given the specific timeframe for the EPA criteria, all those cases have to be classified ninety days prior to the date form which they were originally scheduled. What EPA does is open a floodgate on our normally, otherwise, crowded parole dockets. But on the other hand, this also means that extra work requires overtime pay. And I know for myself that at least that would be comforting for us all to know. But keep in mind that the purpose for that executive order was to relieve overcrowding. And priority number one of the agency at this stage in the game is to relieve overcrowding. In addition, please scan your caseloads for packages that meet the criteria for federal transfers. We are targeting approximately 700 inmates eligible for transfer. And we need those packages done as well. Transfers will be designated for Northeast, Ohio Correctional institute, Youngstown, Ohio Correctional Facility, Red Onion, Virginia, FCI, Sussex I, II, Waverly, Virginia, FCI. Any questions? Thank you. Well, okay, everybody let's get to work right away!

"Attention, attention please, folks, let me have your attention!

"And I almost forgot. Ms Carleen, you have been reassigned to Maximum Security Facility, as of the close of business day. You must report there tomorrow morning 0800 hours. That is all.

Thank you!"

BOBBY JENNINGS AND COCOA BUTTER: Now, Bobby had already made arrangements with Smokie to pick up the merchandise from the chapel at choir rehearsal on Friday, for testing (first twenty-four). They did meet at the chapel and Bobby made the drop. But Bobby took his stash off the top before he met with Smokie because he had set up several deals that were already schedule to move on yesterday, so he was behind already. All he knew was that he had to move and move real fast. As he sat inside the backroom of the chapel with his main man, Cocoa Butter, they discussed how much were to be scored on their first deal. Bobby sat crouched down on a small stool, rambling through a duffle bag that he had laid out on the cement floor. Hence, they both quickly realized that they had in their possession the hottest ticketed item on the pound, given the fact that that new drug was still balling out there (in high demand). With that being said, that K2 had them niggas willing to pay anything for it. For some reason, by Cocoa Butter, being a known druggie connoisseur, he just had to try it too. So Cocoa Butter said "Yo man, you talk a good ass game, but let me sample that k-two, k-three shit, 'cause I gotta rock it one time, just one time. I just wanna fly to the moon man, just one time." Just talking about it, got Bobby to thinking about riding the mother of all highs up to the sky blue yonders "So you really want to try this here shit out?" Then barking right back with a sharp reply. Cocoa Butter said, "You damn right." Actually, Bobby was already hyped and curious himself, so he hurriedly reached into his wallet and took out a wrap for them both to share. He then packed, slapped, and rolled that joint in half sec flat. As Cocoa Butter watched him, he lit up the joint, and passed it to him to hit. So he lunged forward and grabbed the joint from Bobby's hand. His reflexes wouldn't let him wait any longer. So when he got it, he pulled it straight to his mouth and drew the smoke into his chest. He felt the lungs expand. And then he slowly digressed, with the exhale of a halo that fathom a wreath of smoke. Man, we both just sat there on automatic cruise pilot. We both took another slow drag from the joint. In fact, we had lost the will power to control our choices in the matter. This powerful drug took control and beckoned our calls. At first, it seemed so smooth. We got an instant high. I mean like to the moon high 'cause we ain't never seen or felt nothing on earth like it before. But by the time we hit it, a second round, both our jaws were locked, we began to hyperventilate, soon muscle spasms took over, then noses bleed, airways **collapsed** and blood pressure sky rocketed. At that point, our bodily functions, short-circuited, heart rates exploded off the charts, bodies succumbed to shock, breathing ceased, the lights went out. It might be safe to say that within about three to five minutes both were gone. From there, time passed until rehearsal was over. And at the conclusion of rehearsal (several hours later), inmate Coolie came to the back room to lock-up the building, and found two (2) individuals passed out. He immediately alerted the officer. And the officer notified control center by calling a code blue to have all available officers report to the chapel. This was just horrible news for all the prison, both inmate and staff as well. These two people were well known all over the Lorton prison. Everybody liked both Bobby and Cocoa Butter. The alarms were sounded. Also, the medical emergency 911 ambulances were called, state and federal law enforcement, along with the Federal Bureau of Investigation (FBI). This was a fierce investigation. It was very thorough and aggressive. The entire Occoquan Facility remained on lock-down for approximately two weeks. The Prison Emergency Response Teams (PERT) were called and they searched the entire compound, along with their canine (k-9) units, patrolling the dormitories for all contraband. It took about a week for law enforcement to make its determination that a batch of bad drugs had found its way down to Lorton. It didn't take them too long after that to turn up Jimmy Black's name as their prime suspect. Now, at the point of being tagged, Jimmy had to be immediately transferred pending investigation.

CARLEEN ARRIVES AT MAXIMUM SECURITY:

My sentiments about the transfer to maximum security infuriated me at first. I felt that they were trying to set me up for being a fall guy or something else Machiavellian. But when looking at the whole picture, you can appreciate them using some finesse about the scheme of things. I know that it's often lost in the mix, but let's not forget that Lorton has been under mandate for closure and that the department continues to carry out that directive in spite of the challenges it faces. Nevertheless, my transfer to Maximum Security went over without a hitch. I arrived there in April 1998. But I knew immediately that I would miss the quack. Now, many of the changes in the department resulted from an eminent stance that came about from the transition that ushered in the mandate for closure. Although not evident, large numbers of inmates were being shipped out intermittently. On the other hand, staff members were leaving inadvertently for other positions, retirement and/or resigned. From there, we are beginning now to see numerous facilities shutdown as well. In fact, shortly after I left the Occoquan Facility (i.e., the quack), the following year it shutdown in May 1999. As previously mentioned, I was transferred to Maximum Security in April 1998. Upon arrival, I was assigned to the Intake/orientation unit. I supervised the operation of that unit for approximately eighteen months. I was responsible for the classification and housing of every inmate that arrived at Maximum Security within seventy-two hours of arrival. Initially, working there was very difficult. I mean, at first, I felt completely alone because from what I encountered, none of the staff appeared to be team players. They were seemingly hostile from a verbal standpoint, mostly rude, non-congenital, and extremely territorial. However, after several weeks on the job, I finally met my supervisor, **Mr. Jeffery Blunt**. He seemed receptive toward the crucial needs of the unit as a whole, and eager to resolve conflict. Then, most importantly, he was around my age, so I had someone with whom that I could at least identify with or perhaps relate to. For the most part, the staff at Max or as Lorton refers to as "behind the wall" was much older and disgruntled to say the least. But the work was fast pace and fierce, so there was just no time or enough space to walk around carrying a torch all day.

From what I could see, too many people had personal issues that they all somehow related to the job as being the primary culprit for which to blame. If you factored into that the closure, with people being laid off every other week, or staff being reassigned constantly and along with that being denied promotions than you could see why people had a chip on their shoulders. So it was really hard to get things done on a professional level. And whenever you tried, you were labeled as a "know it all," and if you went the extra mile and tried a little harder than you were labeled as a "troublemaker." So most of the time, you couldn't win for losing. For the most part, it was very difficult environment to work in from the beginning, especially without any allies (i.e., behind the wall). So I just took it in stride and did my job. Quite frankly, I felt confident in my ability to do my job, so I could stand on my own. My responsibilities were the assembling of team members for classification committees in order to facilitate the housing process. The members for the most part consisted of personnel from security operations, educational services and mental health professionals. Furthermore, I computed and reviewed security designation profiles whereby determinations were made for proper housing requirements. In addition, I researched and analyzed large amounts of background data, which in turn was utilized to formulate program assessments and recommend treatment referrals. I disseminated written orientation materials, delivered and presented a comprehensive review of institutional rules and regulations per departmental directives. I also established subsequent housing and/ or classification hearings. Now, with that being said, I was the first case manager that an inmate was introduced to upon his arrival at the Maximum Security Facility. I would review volumes of his background data prior to an introduction. I had strict guideline protocols that were setup for housing assignments. In fact, the format went as follows:

MAXIMUM SECURITY HOUSING STATUSES:

CATEGORY	STATUS	ASSESSMENTS	CELLBLOCK
Administrative Segregation	A/S	NEW ARRIVALS/ INTAKES	CB 2,4,6
Protective Custody	PC	VOLU NTARY/INVOLUTARY	CB 1,3,5
Less Restricted Housing	LRH	CLASSIFICATIONS REQUIRED	CB 7
Total Separation	T/S	NO CONTACT PER APPROVAL	CONTROL CELLS
Special Handling	S/H	RESTRICTED CONTACT	CONTROL CELLS
Isolated Status	I/A	RESTRICTED CONTACT	CB 1,3.5
Limited Status	L/S	RESTRICTED CONTACT	CB 2,4.6
Seventy-Two Hours	A/S	INTAKE/ORIENTATION	CB 6-ONLY
Disciplinary transfer	DA	CLASSIFICATION REQUIRED	CB 6
Deadlock	**D/L**	**NO CONTACT PER APPROVAL**	**CONTROL CELLS**

It is also significant to note that the assignments for the recreation and shower schedules were posted for each shift with guidelines for terse protocol. Therefore, everyone assigned to work within the confines of a particular unit should have been on the same page, or singing from the same sheet of music. But in the real world that simply did not happen. In fact, occasionally, a mishap would happen time and time again, whereby, staff could not agree with schedules being assigned at Maximum Security, specifically regarding recreation/shower. Please be advised that housing hearings were conducted per diem per client, every thirty, sixty, and ninety days, which sanctioned compliance with departmental policy. It was during the course of these housing hearings that committee members along with the board chairman would make the inmates' housing statuses and living requirements clear to custodial staff. It is significant to note that any mentioning of compliance with the court ordered consent decree for the Twelve John Doe Lorton Inmates vs. D.C. Department of Corrections at Maximum Security Facility refers to the rights of the inmates to be governed the thirty, sixty, ninety day housing requirements. Note: These guidelines were nonnegotiable.

Also recently a new memorandum came out from the Warden at Maximum Security which reassessed all housing statuses and banned the use of ALL other housing statuses except three. And those three were Administrative Segregation (A/S) which were housed in cellblocks 2, 4, and 6. Then, the Administrative Segregation/ Protective Custody (AS/PC) which were housed in cellblocks 1, 3, and 5. And last but not least, the General Population(G/P) statuses which were housed in cellblock 7. In addition, Total Separation and Special Handlings were considered management designation that could only be authorized by a Deputy Warden or above. **The changes from the housing statuses were primarily generated behind several lawsuits that were being brought against the Department by Lorton inmates at Maximum Security for bogus housing statuses being applied disparately across the board.** Finally, the department lost the lawsuits, and the statuses had to be disbanded. Nevertheless, due to much of the downsizing THAT GENERATED FEDERAL TRANSFERS, along with the closure mandated by THE **NATIONAL CAPITAL REVITALIZATION AND SELF-GOVERNMENT IMPROVEMENT ACT OF 1997,** many of the inmates that were once housed at Maximum Security had subsequently been transferred. Therefore, much of the current population did not need the statues that were banned anyway. So, these were some of the new changes that were generated from

Maximum Security shortly after my arrival on the team. Yet, the hard work at Maximum Security continued its' course. In fact, an outline of all the duties that were able to be accomplished at Maximum Security are listed in the following course of activities. In fact, many of these activities will also highlight some of the ongoing challenges that I encountered while at Maximum Security. The overall itinerary went something similar to the following:

CATEGORY I: QUANTITY OF WORK

The total amount of work actually performed in this particular area was monumental in scope. This becomes relevant when the perspective of the amount of work assessed in the intake cellblock (CB-6) was then compared to the workload requirements of the other cellblocks. For the record, from April 1998 to September 1998, I was basically accompanied by my supervisor, Mr. Jeffery Blunt with meeting the mandated requirements (i.e., learning the operations) for the Intake/Orientation Unit. However, in October 1998, Mr. Blunt was reassigned. From there, be advised that Intake/Orientation was left under the supervision of just one person, Ms. Carleen Williams. So I, Ms. Carleen Williams, assumed the responsibility of the Intake/Orientation Unit which subsequently amassed the following cited below:

September 1998 (total forty-two intakes), October 1998 (total twenty-five intakes), November 1998 (total seventy-six intakes), December 1998 (total twenty-three intakes), January 1999 (total eighteen intakes), February 1999 (total thirty-six intakes), March 1999 (total seventy-five intakes), April 1999 (total 133 intakes), May 1999 (total sixty-seven intakes), June 1999 (total thirty-seven intakes).

4. Approximately **532 intakes** for CB-6
5. Each record must be thoroughly reviewed and screened
6. Secure housing status requirements/security designations
7. Separation Orders
8. Escape history
9. Suspense critical dates
10. Threat to self and/or others
11. Making work folders requires: face sheet 1 & 2, judgment and commitment orders, presentence report, disciplinary reports (within the last year), separation orders, pending charges, security designations, classifications, housing hearings, parole hearings, notification of transfer forms, emergency contacts, etc.

12. In addition, the Intake/Orientation Unit requires routine case management services which include the same services routinely provided by case managers assigned to the other cellblocks as well. The Intake/Orientation Unit (CB-6) was provided with the same services other case managers performed for their cellblocks. Hence, CB-6 received progress reports sent to the U.S. Parole Commission, packages for community services placement, interinstitutional transfers, Federal Bureau of Prison (FOP) security designation, compliance mandates with **Jeffery Jackson, et al. vs. District of Columbia** (thirty, sixty, ninety days housing hearing via court ordered), special housing requirements, legal phone calls, daily monitoring of caseload movement sheets, daily tour of cellblock tiers, routinely prepared **out-of-compliance progress reports**. In addition, whenever, intakes were placed in cellblocks other than the intake block (CB-6) due to lack of bed space (i.e., routinely reports to cellblocks 1, 2, 3, 4, 5, and controlled cells to conduct intake orientation). Also, executed the certificates of conditions of mandatory releases (i.e., secure required signatures). Furthermore, participates in the assignments to adjustment board as committee member, conducts inspections of housing units, process parole notice of actions (i.e., PNOA), classification for detail assignment/removals, facilitates the processing of visiting approval list, handle emergencies and/or concerns that affects the health, safety, and/or welfare of one's overall livelihood. Also, process items that related to seriously ill family members and/or death notices which might generate approval of paper work authorizing a special visit or escorted trip.

13. Records will reflect that routine **task were assigned** to all staff at Maximum Security including (CB-6) regardless of the volumes of intakes that arrived. **Ideally, the inmates would arrive to CB-6, and within seventy-two hours, they were processed for initial orientation interviews. At first, their work folders made, and then housing assessments along with program assessments and/ or treatment referrals followed. From there, classifications were promptly scheduled prior to the close of the next business day. After that, the inmate would be placed in their newly assigned housing status pending bed space. Upon placement, I would forward the inmate's working folder to the perspective case managers. Because CB-6 was considered an Intake/Orientation block, this same format would repeat itself over and over again.**

14. May 1, 1998—Case Managers were sent to cellblocks to notify inmates of new sentence computations, court ordered by the noble decision.

15. June 10, 1998—Adjustment Board Committee (i.e., committee member)
16. June 17, 1998—Reported to Lorton Training Academy for Federal progress report writing
17. July 1, 1998—Adjustment Board Committee
18. July 21, 1998—Adjustment Board Committee
19. September 9, 1998—Special Project for the submission of Federal Bureau of Prison security designation form
20. October 2, 1998—Adjustment Board Committee
21. October 8, 1998—Special Project required
22. October 23, 1998—Adjustment Board Committee
23. October 26, 1998—Adjustment Board Committee
24. November 4, 1998—Adjustment Board Committee
25. December 1, 1998—Adjustment Board Committee
26. December 10, 1998—Adjustment Board Committee
27. December 14, 1998—Adjustment Board Committee
28. December 21, 1998—Adjustment Board Committee
29. December 22, 1998—Special Project required the completion of 187 transfer packages for Youngstown, Ohio
30. January 14, 1999—Adjustment Board Committee
31. January 21, 1999—Adjustment Board Committee
32. January 25, 1999—Special Project due for the completion of inmate profiles
33. February 1, 1999—Adjustment Board Committee
34. February 22, 1999—Adjustment Board Committee
35. March 4, 1999—Assigned daily Unit Inspections (CB-4 Wednesdays)
36. March 19, 1999—Special Project required for the completion of progress reports for inmates transfer to Sussex, Virginia
37. March 31, 1999—Special Project for the completion of Inter-institutional transfers
38. April 5, 1999—Special Project for transfers to Red, Onion, Virginia
39. April 14, 1999—Special Project for transfers to Federal Bureau of Prisons
40. April 16, 1999—Adjustment Board Committee
41. May 18, 1999—Adjustment Board Committee
42. June 9, 1999—Adjustment Board Committee
43. **NOTE: THE ADJUSTMENT BOARD COMMITTTEE WAS AN ALL DAY ASSIGNMENT, AND THIS MEANT UNFORTUNATELY THAT CLASSIFICATIONS/HOUSING HEARINGS WERE RESCHEDULED. THEREFORE COMPROMISING JEFFERY JACKSON, ET. AL VS DISTRICT OF COLUMBIA.**

CATEGORY II: PROBLEMATIC WORKPLACE CONCERNS:

A. Reportedly, rumors were circulated about inmates not being classified within the seventy-two hour guidelines. However, a review of classification materials for CB-6 indicates that inmates were being classified within the seventy-two-hour guidelines. Yet, the officers in CB-6 refused to change the inmate's housing status. Given the extent of this ongoing, systemic, problematic concern, this issue was promptly referred to my supervisor, then **Ms. Ulmar Wiley.** To date, the officers continued to maintain bogus housing statuses for inmates in CB-6 (see D.O. 4350. 2C). It became rather odious to surmise that security/ operations had their own separate agenda, yet, not that far-fetched given this climate of anomie. Although management has been made aware, no corrective measures have been taken per this report.

B. Classification/Housing hearings are routinely cancelled and/or rescheduled primarily due to conflict with employees' leave statuses. In fact, a classification could not convene without a representative from psychological services. If staff psychologist were not available then efforts to secure an alternate staff psychologist was highly improbable (i.e., disrupts assigned schedule causing some to go twice in order to cover for an absent staff psychologist). Meanwhile, no classifications could take place. The classification committee required a representative from security/operations, case management services, psychological services, academic school/educational services, and/or other staff as deemed appropriate. And the unit manager as the chairperson or his/her designee (see D.O. 4350.2 2C). But more importantly, if no psychologist, then no classifications were permitted.

C. Also, there was no accountability within the ranks of clerical and/or support services. Upon submission of a progress report through the routing slip / chain-of-command, no authority would supervise the process by which your product was returned. This particular method promoted cronyism/favoritism which not be tolerated at any level within this organization. Management has been repeatedly informed regarding this matter.

D. Problematic concerns remain prevalent due to inmates being routinely transferred to CB-6 without paperwork from shift supervisors to justify their housing statuses. I have notified my supervisor, Ms. Ulmar Wiley, on numerous occasions regarding this matter. Yet, this same issue has never been resolved.

E. For the record, intakes/new arrivals are not always placed in CB-6. They were often placed wherever there is bed space available. My supervisor was informed repeatedly both verbally and written that this ongoing practice must be stopped immediately. This procedure disrupts the classification orientation process. Again, my supervisor, Ms. Ulmar Wiley, has been informed of these complaints.

F. Furthermore, classifying inmates in cellblock (CBP-6) within the officer's control area is a security breach. It lacks privacy and confidentiality for both staff and inmate. In spite of all the challenges that were encountered via managerial concerns, I have continued to perform and deliver required case management services. And even though there are departmental orders that govern the operational procedures at Maximum Security Facility, in reality, departmental orders are routinely compromised by way of dysfunctional managerial protocol.

G. Upon review in this highly charged condescending emblematic disingenuous workplace, certain staff used their discretion to manipulate rules of engagement in order to carry out elements of personal agendas in the workplace.

H. So instead of the therapeutic methods being utilized in order to assimilate behavior modification theories, measures were being contrived to implore retaliation and/or punishment for misconduct. Hence, in certain cases, without justification inmates' housing statuses were altered. Consequently, unprofessional conduct in the workplace.

CATEGORY III: PERSONAL RELATIONS

Technically, given the manner in which I have performed the duties and responsibilities to meet the mandated requirements in CB-6, I believe that I have extended that same standard of courtesy and respect to others. Again, I have not encountered any documentation that would suggest otherwise per this report.

CATEGORY IV: ADAPTABILITY

During my entire tour of duty with this agency, I have learned nothing but adversity and transition. I am very competent in the performance of my duties and welcome each challenge with commitment and dedication throughout the completion of its task. Since being assigned to the Maximum Security Facility, Intake/Orientation (CB-6), I have demonstrated my ability to deal with many new and diverse situations. For the record, I have conquered each new task and helped resolved multifaceted issues of great duress experienced by the inmate population. In fact, concerns were addressed within the scope of specific areas cited below:

1. Reports to Federal Bureau of Prisons (FBOP) parole hearing
2. Special projects assignments
3. Lorton Training Academy
4. Communicates/translates technical materials for inmates
5. Monitors program goals and therapeutic requirements
6. Corresponds with public and private agencies
7. Addresses out-of-compliance cases (both inherent cases/newly arrivals)
8. Classifications for housing assignments, program assessments, and treatment referrals
9. Addresses emergency transfer concern for treats to safety (i.e., self and others)

Next, the draw down for Maximum Security had turned its final course. It was evident upon my arrival that the inmate population was on a downward slope careening toward a spiral decline, which reaffirmed total compliance with mandates for the Lorton closure plan. Hence, the population at Maximum Security had begun to drop steadily, dwindling week by week. From there, the federal transfers had begun conducting their operations as routine protocol by (1/1999-9/2000) at least once a week. Reportedly, at this point, the bus loads would often transfer out approximately (seventy-five to one hundred) inmates per load, all headed for federal designations. Nevertheless, a large portion of our population behind the wall was harder to designate. And this was primarily due to the fact that much of the inmate population was increasingly older and **wreaked** with serious medical concerns (i.e., physical and mental). Reportedly, there was a case involving an inmate that was transferred from DOC to Red Onion, Virginia in April 2001, without an adequate supply of his medications. And when his medication(s) allegedly ran out, he suffered complications and passed away. In addition, some inmates suffered brutal injuries allegedly while in the custody of federal detainees primarily due to being without their daily-prescribed psychotropic medications. Unfortunately, incidents described such as these brought about major lawsuits by the inmates and their attorneys against the DOC. This created more hurdles and challenges for the Department of Corrections to overcome, consequently, precluding several opportunities for targeted closure dates. However, with continued pursuit of the task given at hand, the Department of Corrections made good on these challenges. And at some point, the inmates at Maximum

Security had all been transferred to federal designations. Therefore, the only facility that remained open at the D.C. Department of Corrections at the Lorton Complex was the Central Facility. Shortly after that, I was assigned to the **Closure team at the Maximum Security.** The Closure team represented a group of staff selected by the Warden to oversee the closure process. We were primarily responsible for the mandates that oversee departmental directives for auditing the administrative/managerial policy review. Finally, we successfully completed that mission and closed the Maximum Security Facility in **February 2001.** After that, I was transferred to the **Correctional Treatment Facility (CTF), a private contract facility ran by Corrections Corporation of America (CCA) for the Department of Corrections (DOC).** I was assigned to the headquarters division of Office of Case Management Services for the Department of Corrections in **March 2001.** It was primarily my responsibility to examine case management materials for clarity, research state prison contracts, analyze guidelines for designations, draft letters, memoranda, generate written and oral correspondence as well. Again, the closure of the Lorton Complex created many new challenges for the D.C. Department of Corrections. Nevertheless, while assigned to case management services, it was my responsibility to screen the inmate population for impediments and/or blockades that precluded transfers. Hence, daily monitoring, constant auditing, tracking and follow up were methods that I employed. I routinely visited the prison cites (i.e., D.C. Jail, Correctional Treatment Facility (CTF), and Central Facility) that remained opened, and conducted extensive reviews of inmates' files in order to identify transfer impediments with the hope of clearing the way for a federal designation. And from there, hopefully expedite clearances for federal designations and/or transfers. As a caseworker for the Headquarters Division for the Department of Corrections Case Management Services, our team was referred to as the "Closure." For the record, we toured the Lorton Complex to make the final assessments for security designation profiles in order to get all of the inmates designated for federal transfer. Our efforts toward this goal were to comply with the newly established law by the congress, which mandated the closure of the Lorton Complex. Hence, this newly drafted legislation became known as the "National Capital Revitalization Act of 1997." I also generated the transport of inmates throughout state contract facilities in order to ensure that deadlines and renewal mandates were not compromised. In addition, I would schedule transport tickets that warranted travel to and fro throughout both state and federal facilities, in order for inmates to appear for their court dates, parole dates, mandatory release dates, etc. Again, there were other various concerns that generated their return to the District as well. There were cases of alleged assaults that prompted subpoenas, depositions, courts dates, while others had medical emergencies, and/or therapeutic mental health issues, etc. I also was required to immediately secure designations for newly arrived inmates as needed and tracked their housing statuses due to the Lorton prisons being mandated for closure in December 2001. In addition, I generated correspondence to concerned family members, government officials, parole board officials, community services volunteers, attorneys, courts, etc., on behalf of the inmates' specific concerns and/or efforts to resolve specific needs.

Jimmy being just plucked up out of his bed in the wee hours of the night, sent shock waves through his world. He had no idea what this unprovoked onslaught of savage attacks on his person was all about. In fact, this was his year to be released. He had already served all his three years and then some, and his time was up. Now, why bring him into this confrontation right now, right at the time when he's due to be released. Jimmy was initially strip searched, held without food or clothing, held in four point restraints, and denied due process rights. From there, his legal visits and/or legal calls were not permitted. After that, he was sent to West Virginia, Atlanta, Georgia, Red Onion, Virginia, Lompac, California, Youngstown, Ohio, etc. So this whole situation left jimmy devastated. He had heard about the fate of his two best friends before he left the quack. He was truly hurt behind the whole scene. He wished he could have changed what happened, but he couldn't. He just had to keep moving forward. All of this comes down to trust as well. He thought he could trust Bobby to be a man of his word, in that, he felt that he could trust Bobby to do what he had promised. He had never had a reason to think otherwise. But then again, he wasn't aware that Bobby was using. He had suspected that something had gone awry, when he cut a backdoor deal. He wished he had just spoke up and shut it down, but he didn't. So for that, he blamed himself. It became hard for Jimmy to keep track of the days of the week in the dark of his jail cell. It became even more difficult for him to determine his location in that his transfer was always done in the early morning hours. He was always held on admin segregation and never in general population. He was locked down 24/7. All of this was done without justification. Then, I found my lawyer address one day. And wrote him a letter. From the get go, I knew I was up a creek without a paddle so I made every effort to be extra kind. Although deep inside, I just wanted to explode and tear that whole place down. With the power of God, he kept me together, he gave me the strength to carry on. Then, I thought to myself, self you need to pray. And I prayed, "Dear, Lord, forgive me, Father, for I have failed time and time again. Father, stretch forth thine hand and draw me unto thee. Help me, Lord to explore higher heights, examine deeper depths, and corral the lowest of my lows. Relieve me of the stench of despair. Forgive me for I count myself the lest of these worthy of thy favor amongst all men that have gone before me. I digress." So after bout nine months, I won some the battles, but, not yet, the war. I finally was able to write and call my mom. She did the work to get hold of my attorney. From there, the ball started to roll. See, I was not able to get my mail at first. In fact, I was transferred so many times that my mail never caught up with my locations. This was no doubt a painful period in my life. I felt all alone in the world. There were even times when I thought I would never be allowed to see my family again. The mere thought of my baby girl made me cry. I felt lost, I felt sad, I felt alone. This half of a man, not whole, but missing strength absent of dignity and human pride. This shell of a man leaning toward the burrows of a brazen cliff, sinking in the hallows of quicksand beneath the murky shores on the banks of rivers so deep. This shell of a man absent of time, and space, yet, baron, and wounded seeking a reason to inhabit a legitimate place. These long quiet dreary days were so lonely, hence, causing my heart to skip regular beats, making every breath labored to say the least. My mind stayed on the edge, racked with crazy thoughts of destruction and mayhem. During that time, I just wanted to explode with grief and pain inside wherever thoughts veered back to the plight of my circumstances. How do I begin to fight an opponent that generates energy from a figment of one's own imagination? I thought I would always feel the warmth of human touch. For all of God's creatures want to be loved, it is also the flowers, the birds, the trees, the animals both land and sea, all of nature long for the admiration of some other compassion of the human species. I have been without the compassion of another for so long that I no longer desire the warmth of human touch. You see, I cried out for a warm touch, prayed for human touch, longed for human touch, until I rid myself of the desire of any human touch. But I do know that we all get weary sometimes. And I know that we cannot always be concerned or troubled by the affairs of this world. I do know that God has control over every piece of fabric that's stitched by his hand. And that we cannot know all of his rhymes or reasons for the master's plan. All we have to do is stand. I don't want my baby girl to think for one minute that I gave up. I want to keep the fight for the future and the legacy of my family alive too. So I live again another day, to keep the struggle alive. And with that being said, I popped off a letter to my attorney, and primarily explained my situation.

JAIL HOUSE LETTER:

According to Jimmy, this was the most important letter of his life. Almost immediately, he tried to recant the lesson plans from his high school teacher about punctuation and grammar. He prayed to God earnestly to get him through this experience and that he would return to school for a formal education and improve his relentless quest for knowledge. 'Cause up until this point for him, it's all been fun and games, but now he wanted to take his education seriously. So he settled down and gathered his thoughts and began to write his attorney a letter. So Jimmy started out explaining what he wanted to convey, yet by the end of the letter, he literally uses first person diction to speak exactly what he wants.

Dear Mr. Alex Hershel,

I think my current situation explains better about how my violations occurred than I could ever explore.

All of this convoluted entrapment style police tactic violated my civil rights under the constitution. Yet, to no avail, my plea has continued to fall on deaf ears. I first explained about how they violated my due process rights under the law, and commenced to lock me down 24/7 without my due process rights. Then, I was implicated in the deaths of two that overdosed on a drug scam. In addition, they threw drugs charges on me for possession, distribution, manufacturing, a drug enterprise, yet, they have no evidence whatsoever. Except the word of a crack head, now give me a break. Also, my property was then confiscated and destroyed. All of my mail from my family have traveled across several states, yet, most of it has never reached my locations. In most cases, by the time my mail arrives, I get transferred out. Man, this crap has got to stop. Please, fix that man, please find my mail. Then, I ask this as another favor, I want to ask of you, please. Most of everybody I know are becoming like ghost, man, they all just appear to be checking out, like punching a clock. Anyway, man can you find out what ever happened to some buddies of mine. Tell me all you can find out about Cecil Sutton, Marlow McCoy, and Larmar Taylor. At some point, we were all serving time at Lorton for this same bit that we doing time for right now. Can you do something about this lockdown move that they perpetrated on me. Being my judge, jury, and executioner without a trial. Well, that's all for now, thanks man!

Later, sign.

Jimmy.

Mr. Alex Hershel, now with two promotions under his belt, is now Assistant District Attorney for the District of Columbia.

FEDERAL BUREAU OF PRISONS (FOP) HOUSING DESIGNATIONS

There was intense confrontation about the overall facility assignments that prompted the federal transfers at the Lorton Complex. The whole process had to be realigned. The D.C. inmates and their families got together and filed numerous lawsuits in D.C. Superior Courts against the Federal Bureau of Prisons for improper designations which their attorneys cited ongoing systemic errors in federal housing assessments that resulted in brutal assaults, and in some cases murder. There were several inmates that were sent to the same facilities and were not properly designated, and were murdered by rival groups of inmates, most of whom were improperly housed as well. So much tension exploded between both sides of the aisle that each side vowed not to give an inch to the other. These court battles were highly charged and fiercely brutal. Neither side wanted to let up on their litigations before the court nor each fought hard to set precedent in the ongoing fights to win their cases. Each court ruling just simply set the stage for what prompted one appeal after the other. The road to a final disposition appeared to be nowhere in sight. So the battle continued despite of the fact that the instrument being used to designate Federal transfers remained under litigation before the courts.

TAHOE BLANGO:

My whole family misses Jimmy. We pray for him and the return of his safety every night. I write letters faithfully, but, Jimmy never writes back. I was obviously concerned by the daunting lapse of time that it was taking to get some information regarding his whereabouts. I called the prison at Occoquan Facility and they said that he had been transferred. Then, one of his friends got word to me that he was transferred due to the death of two crack heads at Lorton. They said that the prison officials had got a snitch to rat out Jimmy on the drug sell. So Jimmy had to be moved for his own safety. Anyway, all of this just sounds stupid to me. It just don't make no sense. Jimmy is a born leader and he's not a follower. He stands for pride, unity, and brotherhood. This is the true essence of my son and what he represents wherever he goes. So all that the prison guards were telling me about Jimmy was just nonsense. Aside from all that, I asked of them what evidence did they have to prove that what they were saying was true. To date, they have not been able to produce any legitimate evidence that supports their claims. At this point, all they have is third party hearsay and no facts. So I am asking all parties involved, why can't Jimmy come home? From there, Mr. Hershel, Jimmy's attorney started the ball rolling. Although it seemed like progress was slow, eventually some success began to start paying off.

ASSISTANT DISTRICT ATTORNEY FOR DISTRICT OF COLUMBIA. MR. ALEX HERSHEL

Upon receipt of Jimmy's letter, Mr. Hershel went straight to work on Jimmy's behalf. He had been aware of the litany of court case appeals carried out by the DCDC Department of Corrections and the United States Federal Parole Commission. Both entities were in the fight to settle the dispute once and for all as to who had the authority to designate inmates from the District of Columbia, once they were recommended for federal transfer. Well, each agency had their own instrument and each one claimed that their instrument superceded the jurisdiction of the other. They also argued over the quality of their opponent's instruments and how the data was being utilized. Again, each one claimed that theirs were better than the other one. This battle was quite frankly fierce to say the least. And by now, both agencies had litigated their cases all the way to the United States Supreme Court, the highest court in the land. So with each side, eagerly waiting for the courts to rule on their behalf, everybody was on edge. Although Mr. Hershel was not directly involved in the case between the Federal United States Parole Commission and the DCDC Department of Corrections, he watched eagerly for its outcome. For he knew that this final court decision would affect the lives of many of his clients confined at the Lorton Complex as well.

FEDERAL BUREAU OF PRISONS (FOP) SECURITY DESIGNATIONS:

This convoluted battle over **SECURITY DESIGNATIONS** were fought long and hard and without an end game in sight. However, no prejudices were found to be involved, just the basic arguments for legitimate guidelines and sounds principals. Hence, each one leaned hard on the other. A review of the specific dialogue, whereas the content of the federal documents were being challenged by the DCDC documents for legitimacy and clarity remains sharply divided. Both sides were at a stalemate over almost every aspect of the documents as a whole when it came to challenges presented by their opponent. In addition, it remained a dilemma as to when and how one's discretion should be applied in resolving their dispute. For now, the courts continued their proceedings and allowed both agencies to present their closing arguments before the judge explaining why their agency should be the last AND FINAL AUTHORITY OVER security designations/ TRANSFERS IN THE DISTRICT OF COLUMBIA.

Again, the closure of the Lorton Complex was prompted by the National Capital Revitalization and Self-Government Improvement Act of 1997.

This particular legislation ordered the closure of the Lorton Complex on or December 31, 2001. Therefore, the entire inmate population had to be reclassified and designated for transfer to the Federal Bureau of Prisons. Consequently, the case management staff at the Lorton Complex had to be trained on the Federal Bureau of Prison's 1996 manual, signifying the by laws, regulations and/or administrative procedures for security designation and custody classification (PS 5100.07). For the most part, this security designation procedure was similar to our D.C. Department of Corrections classification process at Lorton in that both began within three days or seventy-two hours upon arrival. Reportedly, the Federal Bureau of Prisons catechize an array critical factors pertaining to background and criminal history both of which are thoroughly examined on the security designation form in order to determine proper housing. Upon completion of the security designation form, the inmate will receive his final custody level score. This particular score corresponds to the inmate's custody level requirements. In fact, the final section of the assessment form computes the score that assigns the inmate his final security designation. In addition, there are other factors which are taken into account when inmates are being designated for custody level requirements. Some of these factors include the following according to the Federal Bureau of Prison guidelines.

1. **Security Level**—the security levels are minimum, low, medium, high, and administrative status (i.e., medical/mental health concerns, pretrial, and holdovers).
2. **Public Safety Factors**—this area consist of specific categories which are utilized to ensure the orderly operations of the institutions and the protection of our community as a whole. Now, whenever these areas are found in the criminal profile of an offender, these areas are highlighted on the security designation form via letter code. This letter code will alert staff, whom will in turn apply the appropriate guidelines for custody designation. It is noteworthy that Federal guidelines require that public safety factors be reviewed on a case-by-case basis in order to determine if the category should be waived. In fact, offenders that are flagged for this particular category are not permitted housing at a minimum-security facility unless a waiver is granted. For the record, the category which fall into this particular area include the following:

    a. **Greatest Severity Offense**—This specific category must be reviewed whenever the offender incurs a score within the highest range of point applicable due to the nature of his charge. In other words, if an offender's crime falls within a specific category, due to the nature of the charge, then the housing requirements assigned will accommodate the security measures based on the outcome of the score.

b. **Disruptive Groups**—These individuals have been identified as gang members. Their official files also contain legitimate documentation that supports gang related activity.

c. **Sex offenders**—Each case involved in this category consist of offenders that were charged and convicted of sex related offenses.

d. **Threat to government officials**—In order to highlight this particular category, records must contain evidence that supports the identity of the individual (i.e., classification required via Central Inmate Monitoring System(CIMS). This offender cannot be housed in a minimum custody facility unless he receives a waiver.

e. **Deportable aliens**—This particular category includes offenders who are considered a citizen of a foreign country unless the offender can prove otherwise. The scoring of this category shall not be applied when the Immigration and Naturalization Service (INS) has made the decision to forego deportation proceedings. However, if the offender incurs a score in this particular category, he cannot be housed in a minimum custody facility unless he receives a waiver.

f. **Sentence lengths**—With regard to this category, an offender having ten years or more remaining to serve on the current offense will be qualified for the public safety risk category on the security designation form.

g. **Violent behavior**—The qualifications for this category requires at least two incidents of violence within the past five years. This category also includes serious escapes and prison disturbances.

3. **Sentence limitation**—This concept refers to an offender who was sentenced under certain statues and restrictions which inadvertently affects the offender's placement in an institution. In fact, some of the statues that routinely precludes the offender's placement at certain facilities are listed as follows: Youth Corrections Act (YRA) offenders, misdemeanors, parole violators requiring revocation hearings, study cases requiring medical/mental health evaluations, deportable aliens, court ordered work release participants, and court recommended transfers.

4. **Management Variables**—This concept means that professional discretion was used in the areas of public safety factors whereby

the offender was assigned to a greater security or lesser in order to ensure appropriate housing. In cases where management variables are required, the offender is subsequently housed at a facility that is inconsistent with the custody that he would otherwise require. Furthermore, when management variables are applied, they are analyzed and approved by the regional director or his designee. It is significant to note that the goal of the institution is to house the inmate at the lowest custody level possible, without jeopardizing the orderly operation of the institution and the safety of the community as a whole. For example, there are situation whereby offenders often goes to court and have detainers removed or charges dropped. From there, the offender would be considered as a lesser risk than his current assigned custody level. In such cases, a management variable could be applied. Upon approval, the inmate would be transferred to a lesser security level facility. Therefore, it should be duly noted that multiple custody levels may be housed within the same institution. Nevertheless, the highest custody level assigned to an inmate must not exceed the security level designation established by the institution. Furthermore, in accordance with the Federal Bureau of Prison guidelines for housing requirements, there are specific criteria for scoring each item on the security designation form. For the record, the security designation form contains items that score the following:

A. Severity of Offense—The standard guidelines to follow for this particular score depend on the terms by which the offender was released from custody. In some cases, the offender was released from custody due to serving the entire term of their sentence, resulting in them being mandatory released. On the other hand, some of them were granted parole, whereby compliance with the guidelines of parole supervision were mandatory. However, some offenders served a specific term of incarceration and subsequently incurred special conditions for supervised release. Nevertheless, according to the federal statues for the security designation guidelines, the behavior that returned the offender to custody is the behavior that will be scored. The original behavior that occurred before the incident that returned him to custody is considered past behavior and cannot be used to score the severity of the offense category. However, if new criminal conduct returned him to custody, use the new criminal conduct (i.e., score behavior) without regard for the outcome of his conviction status. On the other hand, if the offender is a newly sentenced inmate, the behavior that resulted in the conviction of the original offense will be scored. The charges incurred are not necessarily the overriding factor that determines the score. Quite frankly, it is the criminal conduct (i.e., illegal activity) or the behavior itself that is considered paramount in determining the severity of the offense code. In addition, if there are multiple charges in play, then the charge that carries the highest severity offense code will be scored.

B. **Detainers**—Federal regulations permit the scoring of detainers only when documentation can be provided to show just cause that the detainer is active. The federal guidelines also scores concurrent sentences as a detainer, but only if it exceeds the federal term currently being served. In addition, federal regulations allows detainers to be scored for the following: consecutive state sentences, pending charges, state parole violation terms, and outstanding warrants.

C. **Public Safety Factors**—These factors are evaluated to determine the need for an increased security status regardless of the inmate's security designation score. As previously indicated, public safety factors are utilized to determine appropriate housing requirements in order to ensure that the security measures employed are not being compromised.

D. **Expected Length of Incarceration**—This score must reflect the total number of months remaining on the inmate's sentence less 15% (sentences over twelve months) plus credit for jail time served (if applicable). If there remains at least ten years or more to serve on the original sentence, then score the item marked public safety factor for length of sentence.

E. **Type of Prior Commitment**—This particular category refers to the offender's entire criminal background. In fact, in order to be scored as a prior commitment, records must indicate that a physical release from custody resulted in a minimum severe offense behavior should be scored as the prior commitment. It is significant to note that points are specifically related to the offense behavior and not to the nature of the charge incurred. Please note that the offense severity scale will assign a particular point for the charges currently being served.

F. **History of escapes or attempts**—The offender's escape history includes the entire background. It also includes any escapes or attempted escapes from confinement or from community services supervision as well. The item in the escape history category will be counted as long as the escape resulted in a conviction. The most recent incident of escape should be scored for items in this category. There are other convictions that can incur points assessed for escape such as Failure to Appear and Bail Reform Act. However, these incidents must have resulted in charges of serious misconduct (i.e., car accidents resulting in death, violation of court decree, and flights to avoid prosecution).

G. **History of Violence**—The points assessed in this category are not to include the charges incurred in the instant offense. The behavior scored in this category will be past maladaptive behavior cited for misconduct. Again, the points assessed in this category include the entire criminal background. To score this particular item, only use incidents of violence that resulted in a conviction or finding of guilt. Most of the information used to score these items were derived from the presentence investigative reports, incident reports, disciplinary reports, court documents, etc. Upon completion of the data collected from a myriad of stats and resources, the information is then calibrated to assess the requirements for the security designation form. Once the form is completed, the offender is assigned security designation score. This score will then notify the offender of his security designation score. And depending on his score, the custody level for that offender would be high, low, medium, minimum, and/or administrative status.

D.C. DEPARTMENT OF CORRECTIONS SECURITY DESIGNATION AND CUSTODY CLASSIFICATION SYSTEM:

The instrument for which the custody levels are determined for D.C. Department of Corrections is called the security designation and custody classification system (D.O. 5010.7). This particular document also determines the offenders housing requirements within the D.C. PRISON system. Now, both agencies claim that their housing assessment form is more sophisticated than the other. This fierce battle between the two has sparks major lawsuits being filed in D.C. Superior Court with litigations having no end in sight. In fact, some of the categories reviewed by the District on the initial classification custody review form are listed as follows:

1. **History Of Institutional Violence**—This area scores the entire background of violent behavior within the scope of five years prior

to the current term of incarceration. In order to score this category the incident must include findings of guilt. Furthermore, incident of assault/attempted assault or bodily injury are scored in this category as well.

2. **Severity Of Current? Offense**—This particular item requires that you score the charges currently being served. If more than one charge is currently being served then the charge which carries the greatest severity level would be deemed appropriate.

3. **Prior Assaultive History**—This section requires that you review the offender's entire criminal background and score assaultive behavior. Assaultive behavior is described as any bodily contact that actually occurred or attempted regardless of an apparent injury. This item will score both prior convictions and parole violations for assaultive behavior. This category also requires a finding of guilt in order to be scored.

4. **Escape history**—In this particular category the escape history refers to the entire criminal history. This item is scored without regards to the inmate's conviction status or criminal prosecution. All documented incidents of escapes are scored. However, remember that the Federal Bureau of Prison (FBOP) will only assess points for escapes that resulted in convictions. And the conviction must be within the last five years.

5. **Time to Earliest Release in Months**—In order to score, this category began with the offender's commitment date. From there, determine the offender's earliest release date (preferably the parole eligibility date). After that, count the number of months that makes up the difference between the two. This will give the number of months that the offender must serve before being considered eligible for release.

6. **Alcohol/Drug History**—This category requires that the presentence investigative report be reviewed in order to determine how much criminal history involved drugs. The points incurred for this category will depend on the number of drug and/or alcohol convictions incurred during the entire course of the criminal career.

7. **Current Detainer**—This item would include detainers that have been formally lodged by the requesting jurisdiction. It is significant to note that pending charges and parole board warrants are considered as detainers.

8. **Prior Felony Convictions**—This item scores all prior felony convictions except the current offense. In this category, all criminal conduct is scored regardless of the date that it occurred.

Once again, the last section of this form will retain a final custody score. This particular score will determine the appropriate housing requirements for DOC inmates at the Lorton Complex. The score will assess a custody level for minimum, medium, high, and low. In my opinion, there are staunch differences between the two agencies, specifically regarding the overall application assessments, default technicalities, and discretionary overrides. A few areas worth making note of would be that DOC uses the criminal offense code that relates to the charges incurred in order to assess a score. (i.e., score points by reviewing the list of charges located on the criminal severity chart). On the other hand, the Federal Bureau of Prisons scores the actual behavior that occurred, using the severity offense scale as oppose to scoring the nature of the charge. In addition, when the FOP scores criminal conduct that involves illegal drugs, they have to specify the amount of drugs that resulted in the conviction for the current offense. Nevertheless, the DOC uses the severity of criminal offense code to score the charges incurred for drug convictions regardless of the actual quantity of drugs involved. These are just a few of the primary factors that account for the differences in the scoring of the data being analyzed. Hence, the overall results of the security levels being assessed makes the difference between whether or not an inmate will be classified as medium, minimum, high, low. And this is crucial to the inmate's livelihood which in some cases could mean the difference between life and death. In fact, the mere custody level alone can cost you your life. Upon receipt of an assignment of close custody, the inmate(s) would be shipped out as priority transfers to West Coast Federal Correctional Institutions. If you are a high custody level, you go to the front the bus. If you are medium custody, you will be shipping out next, filling up the second bus. And so on and so on down the line.

ASSISTANT DISTRICT ATTORNEY MR. ALEX HERSHEL:

Dear Jimmy,

I wish this letter finds you well despite all that you have encountered. It is my best hope that you remain in good health and stay strong. Not only that, I truly regret all that your family have suffered as well. First of all, GOODNEWS, I was successful with the filing of a writ of habeas corpus and the judges have ruled in our favor. Now, as soon as this ink dries on this court ordered release document, you will be on your way back to Washington, D.C. From there, upon YOUR return, you will be released to the D.C. Parole Board AUTHORITY.

I have been able to retrieve most but not all of your mail. However, there are just two other locations left for me to search.

Finally, I have gone through my resources and put together a small posse to work as team on behalf of my quest to expedite this last project (i.e., in order to make good on that last favor), in which I might add was a tall order. And this is how it went down. Thus far, this was all I was able to find . . . see attached. Remember, Jimmy, you owe me for this one man, remember that man. I'm looking forward to seeing you soon.

Family and friends are anxiously awaiting your return!

Wishing you happy travels,

Mr. Alex Hershel,
Assistant District Attorney

CRIMINAL DATA INFORMATION
DOC SUPERIOR COURT
INMATE PROFILE

INMATE NAME: **LARMAR TAYLOR** HEIGHT: 57″
RACE/ETHNICITY: AFRO-AMERICAN WEIGHT: 195
DATE OF BIRTH: 3/12/1974 HAIR COLOR: BLACK
AGE: 24 YRS DCDC#: 221-659 COMPLEXION: BROWN
ALIASES/AKA: CRACK HEAD, NIEMIN MARCUS EYE COLOR: BROWN
TATTOOS/ SCARS: LEFT ARM CROSS/ BACK UNICORN GENDER: MALE
CHARGES: ROBBERY, ATTEMPTED ROBBERY UUV, PLEA: GUILTY
SENTENCE: 25 YEARS TO LIFE ATTORNEY: Y/N
ESCAPES: NONE JUVENILE HISTORY: Y/N
GANG AFFILIATED: DC BLOODS CONVICTED: FELON
SENTENCING JUDGE: JUDGE JOHN MCKINNLEY COURT FEES: WAIVED

CHARGES: ROBBERY, ATTEMPTED ROBBERY, BREAKING AND ENTERING, UNAUTHORIZED USE OF A STOLEN VEHICLE, UNAUTHORIZED POSSESSION OF A STOLEN VEHICLE, POSSESSION OF A CONTROLLED SUBSTANCE (MARIJUANA).

SERVING: 25 YEARS TO LIFE PED: 2-20-2045 STD: 5-23-19 FTD: 7-2-26

NARRATIVE: **INCARCERATED ON 9/14/97** AT LORTON PRISON, YET, RECORDS REFLECT EXTENSIVE CRIMINAL HISTORY. IMMEDIATELY TRANSFERRED TO THE LORTON COMPLEX, VIRGINIA, **CENTRAL FACILITY,** TO SERVE TIME. INITIAL OVERALL ADJUSTMENT DESCRIBED AS MARGINAL AT BEST. THE FIRST SIX MONTHS WERE SPENT IN ADMINISTRATIVE SEGREGATION DUE TO HIS REQUEST FOR PROTECTIVE CUSTODY. REGULARLY RECEIVED COUNSELING AND OFTEN MEDS TO COPE WITH EPISODES AND/OR BOUTS OF BIPOLOAR DEPRESSION.

RELASESED ON GENERAL POPULATION WITHIN THE LAST COUPLE OF YEARS 1998-1999. SEEMINGLY PROGRESSING WELL. MEDICAL HEALTH RELATIVELY STABLIZED. HAS NOT BEEN A DISCIPLINARY PROBLEM WITHIN LAST TWENTY-FOUR MONTHS.

ASSIGNED ACADEMIC/VOCATIONAL SCHOOL, SUBSTANCE ABUSE COUSELING, WORK DETAIL, CLEAR CONDUCT. PER CASE MANAGER, MR. JERRY FISHER, LASTEST INCIDENT INCLUDES: A PRIOR INCIDENT OF DISRESPECT AND LACK OF COOPERATION, CLASS II VIOLATIONS, 1998. FOUND GUILTY, FOURTEEN DAYS ADM/SEG. **SINCE TRANSFERRED TO FCI, TERRA HAUTE, INDIANA, 2000.**

CRIMINAL DATA INFORMATION
DOC SUPERIOR COURT
INMATE PROFILE

INMATE NAME: **CECIL SUTTON** HEIGHT: 5´9˝
RACE/ETHNICITY: AFRO-AMERICAN WEIGHT: 195
DATE OF BIRTH: 11-4-73 HAIR COLOR: BLACK
AGE: 25 YRS DCDC#206-411 COMPLEXION: LIGHT BROWN
ALIASES/AKA: EASY-BREEZY EYE COLOR: BROWN
TATTOOS/SCARS: SKULL AND BONES CHEST GENDER: MALE
CHARGES: CURRENT THREE STRIKES LAWS PLEA: GUILTY
SENTENCE: 45 YRS TO LIFE ATTORNEY: Y/N
ESCAPE: NONE JUVENILE HISTORY: SEALED
GANG AFFILIATED: DCDC BLOODS CONVICTED: FELON
SENTENCING JUDGE: MR. SINCLAIR MCADOO COURT FEES: WAIVED

CHARGES: ROBBERY, ARMED ROBBERY, UNAUTHORIZED USE OF A VEHICLE, BREAKING AND ENTERING, UNAUTHRORIZED USE OF STOLEN VEHICLE, UNAUTHORIZED POSSESSION OF A STOLEN VEHICLE, RESISTING AN ARREST, OBSTRUCTION OF JUSTICE, POSSESSION OF A CONTROLLED SUBSTANCE

SERVINING: 45 YEARS TO LIFE
SHORT TERM DATE: LIFE
FULL TERM DATE: LIFE

NARRATIVE: ARRIVED AT THE **LORTON COMPLEX 5/23/97.** DUE TO HIS LENGTHY CRIMINAL BACKGROUND, THE JUDGE MCCADOO, WAS DIRECTED TO APPLY THE THREE STRIKES LAW UNDER DC CRIMINAL CODE CR2240067 INACTED BY THE UNITED STATES SURPREME COURTS WHICH ESSENTIALLY SAYS THAT THIS INDIVIDUAL HAS AN EXTENSIVE CRIMINAL BACKGROUND AND THE FULL EXTENTOF THE LAW MUST BE APPLIED, HENCE, DEEMED A THREAT TO SOCIETY, HIM SELF AS WELL AS OTHERS. SERVED TIME: **INCARCERATED AT MAXIMUM SECURITY FACILITY 10/15/97.** BEHAVIOR DESCRIBED IN ONE WORD AS INCORRIGIBLE: OVERALL ADJUSTMENT POOR (I.E., RECALCITRANT), RECEIVED THIRTY DISCIPLINARY REPORTS, ADMINISTRATIVE SEGREGATION FORTY TIMES WITHIN EIGHTEEN MONTHS. DESCRIBED AS HAVING

POOR SOCIAL SKILLS, ADULT PREDATOR, STRONG ARMING, ANTISOCIAL PERSONALITY, SOCIOPATH WITH PSYCHOTIC TENDENCIES.

THUS FAR, REFUSES ALL MEDS, COUNSELING, AND/OR TREATMENT DEEMED WALKING TIME BOMB.

AFTER APPROXIMATELY TWO YRS, HE PLOTTED TO REINVENT HIMSELF, THUS, GAINED TRUST FROM STAFF & MANIPULATED AUTHORITY FIGURES. HENCE, 1999, SOLICITED CLERICAL STAFF (ROMATIC AFFAIR) TO REMOVE DISCIPLINARY REPORTS FROM HIS RECORD. GENERATED FRAUDULANT DOCUMENTS THAT QUALIFIED HIM FOR HALFWAY HOUSE PLACEMENT. CONSEQUENTLY, HIS NAME WAS PLACED ON THE TRANSFER DOCKET FOR COMMUNITY SERVICES, HOPE VILLAGE WITH HELP FROM STAFF (ROMATIC AFFAIR). UPON ARRIVAL, **HE ESCAPES. HOOKED UP WITH FORMER GANGBANGERS AND CRACKHEADS.** HE WENT ON A DRUG BINGE, AND WAS HIGH ON DRUGS FOR THREE DAYS—WHEREBY SHORTLY THEREAFTER HE ABDUCTED, ROBBED, AND MURDERED A CAUCASIAN FEMALE AT AN ATM MACHINE IN WASHINGTON, D.C. VICTIM WAS SHOT POINT BLANK RANGE TO THE HEAD (RIGHT TEMPLE LOBE). IN THE FIRST FORTY-EIGHT HRS, THE D.C. POLICE MANHUNT RESULTED IN HIS APPREHENSION, CUSTODY, AND PROSECUTION. FROM THERE, HE WAS FOUND GUILTY IN DC SUPERIOR COURT IN 12/99 AND RECEIVED A SENTENCE OF **LIFE WITHOUT THE POSSIBILITY OF PAROLE. TRANSFERRED TO FCI, LOMPAC, CALIFORNIA, 2001.**

CRIMINAL DATA INFORMATION
DOC SUPERIOR COURT
INMATE PROFILE

INMATE MATE: **MARLOW MCCOY**	HEIGHT: 6´2˝
RACE/ETHNICITY: AFRO-AMERICAN	WEIGHT: 245
DATE OF BIRTH: 6/30/73	HAIR COLOR: BLACK
AGE: 25 YRS DCDC# 203-445	COMPLEXION: DARK BROWN
ALIASES/AKA: NONE	EYE COLOR: BROWN
TATTOOS/SCARS: BACK SPREAD EAGLE, SKULL AND BONES	GENDER: MALE
CHARGES: ROBBERY, UUV, PWID, POSS OF FIREARM	PLEA: GUILTY
SENTENCE: 55 YRS TO LIFE	ATTORNEY: MCCLEAN
ESCAPE: HOPE VILLAGE 3/21/87	JUVENILE HISTORY: Y/N
GANG AFFILIATED: DC BLOODS	CONVICTED: FELON
SENTENCING JUDGE: MR. SARSOLEE	COURT FEES: WAVIED

CHARGES: ROBBERY, ARMED ROBBERY, UNAUTHORIZED USE OF A STOLEN VEHICLE, BREAKING AND ENTERING, UNAUTHORIED USE A VEHICLE, POSSESSION OF A CONTROLLED SUBSTANCE (HERION), ASSAULT ON A POLICE OFFICER RESISTING AN ARREST.

SERVING: 55 YEARS TO LIFE
SHORT TERM DATE: LIFE
FULL TERM DATE: LIFE

NARRATIVE: ARRIVED AT THE **LORTON COMPLEX 11/3/97,** MAXIMUM SECURITY. TO BEGAN SERVING A TERM OF LIFE SENTENCE. OVERALL ADJMENT MARGINAL AT BEST. TREATMENT STAFF FINDINGS: **PSYCHOPATHIC TENTENCIES, SEEKING PERSONAL GAIN, PREDATOR MENTALITY, FIERCE MANIPULATOR.** TRANSFERRED TO OCCOQUAN FACILITY DUE TO OVERCROWDING. HE BEGAN PRISON AFFAIR WITH FEMALE GUARD. THEN, AFTER THREE YEARS, HE PLANNED AND EXECUTED AN ESCAPE. THE FEMALE GUARD WAS AN ACCESSORY BEFORE AND AFTER THE FACT. FEMALE-GUARD AIDEDED AND ABETTED BY PLAYING AN ESSENTCIAL ROLE IN THE PLOT. SHE PLACED A SET OF HER OLD UNIFORMS AT THE CHECKPOINT, SO THAT INMATE MCCOY WOULD BE ALLOWED TO CHANGE HIS PRISON GARB-PUT ON AN OFFICER'S UNIFORM IN

A DISGUISE AND WALK OUT THE FRONT GATE OF THE OCCOQUAN FACILITY. IN 12/99, HE WENT ON ESCAPE AND WAS SUBSEQUENTLY RECAPTURED 9/2000, WHICTHA, KANSAS. UPON RETURN, HE WAS HELD OVER IN ARLINGTON COUNTY VIRGINIA TO WAIVE ETRADICTION, PENDING HIS RETURN TO THE DISTRICT, ON AN ARRAY OF OUTSTANDING FELONY CHARGES WHEN HE ALLEGEDLY TOOK HIS OWN LIFE. HOWEVER, CIRCUMSTANCES SURROUNDING HIS DEATH WERE INCONCLUSIVE—AUTOPSY REPORTS RULED DEATH A HOMICIDE.

This is my first blog. I have lots to learn. I am not too comfortable with gadgets, but I have gotten better. I am interested very much in starting my new project. My new project that I have decided to take on is writing my first book. Can anyone out there feel my pain? So every day, I turn the corner into the unknown. There are no warning signs, stop signs, speed limits, and tollbooths. There's just open highways and I'm lost.

So, as I sat down at the kitchen table to earnestly ponder the gravity of that profound journey traveled that day, this still small voice beckons my call. The windows of time transcends the scope of one's ability to access the choices that are made . . . when given the traffic unknown.

OUR CRIMINAL JUSTICE SYSTEM IS DEFINITELY BROKEN AND HAS BEEN OUT OF CONTROL FOR MANY YEARS. THE STATE OF THE PRISON SYSTEM TODAY IS THE RESULT OF A MULTIFACETED operation THAT HAS SEPARATE AND DISTINCT PARTS THAT has GONE AWRY AND SORELY NEEDS REPAIR. AND LASTLY, ONE OF THE GREATEST MEN OF OUR TIMES ONCE STATED THAT **"CHANGE WILL NOT COME IF WE WAIT FOR SOME OTHER PERSON OR SOME OTHER TIME. WE ARE THE ONES WE'VE BEEN WAITING FOR. WE ARE THE CHANGE THAT WE SEEK."**

PRESIDENT BARACK HUSSEIN OBAMA

BIBLIOGRAPHY

Shin, A.nnys, "Washington City Paper." March 9, 2001, Washington, D.C.

Stansell, Christine, "Suffrage and the South." The New York Times. (2011)

Carver, John, "Using Drug Testing To Reduce Detention." Federal Probation, 00149128, (Mar 1993) Vol 57, Issue 1.

Rafter, Hahn Nicole and Stanley, L Debra, "Prisons In America—A Reference Handbook." Contemporary World Issues.

Herman, G Peter, *The American Prison System*. The H.W. Wilson Company, 2001.

Zimmer, E Lynn, "Women Guarding Men", The University of Chicago Press

Van Wormer, Stuart Katherine and Bartollas, Clemens, "Women And The Criminal Justice System.

Kerman Piper, *Orange Is The New Black-My Year In A Women's Prison*, New York, 2010.

Girshick, B. Lori, "No Safe Haven", Northwestern University Press, Boston, MA. 2003.

District of Columbia: Issues Related to the Youngstown Prison Report and Lorton Closure Process: GGD-00-86, GAO Reports, 4/7/2000, p1, 36p

Arbetma, O'Brien and Mc Mahon. Street Law. New York: West Publishing Company, 1990.

Rush, Jeffery, Probation Officer-Parole Officer Exam United States: Thompson Learning Center Inc, 2000.

Ryan, Daniel Pretrial Release and Detention. Washington, D.C. Administrative Office of United States Courts, 1993.

REFERENCE MATERIALS

Daniel J. Bayse, "As Free As An Eagle." 1991, American Correctional Association, 8025 Laurel Lakes Court, Laurel, Md. 20707-5075

Marian Faux, "The Complete Resume Guide." 1995, Arco Books, A Simon & Schuster Macmillan Company, 1633 Broadway, New York, N.Y. 10019-6785

Jim Niemeier, "From The Inside Out, A Parole Planning Manual." 1991, Interstate Publishers Inc., 510 North Vermillion Street, P.O. Box 50, Danville, Il. 61834-0050

Ned Rollo and Louis W. Adams, "A Map Thorugh The Maze." 1993, OPEN INC., P.O. Box 566025, Dallas, Texas 75356-6025

Ned Rollo, "Man I Need A Job." 1993., OPEN INC., P.O. Box 566 025, Dallas, Texas 75356-6025

Ned Rollo, "99 Days and A Get Up." 1988, OPEN INC., P.O. Box 566025, Dallas, Texas 75356-6025

Errol Craig Sull, "The Ex-Inmate Complete Guide To Successful Employment.", 1990, Aardvark Publishing, 370 Franklin Street, Buffalo, N.Y. 14202.

The Pre-Employment Training Curriculum Package, 1979; The American Correctional Association, 4321 Hartwick Road, College Park, Md. 20740

Biography

I have been blessed to work over twenty-seven years in the prison system for both the Washington, D.C., metropolitan area and the state of North Carolina Department of Corrections. My career began in 1986 upon completion of my college studies in Chapel Hill. I am a product of the North Carolina public school system. I graduated from Kinston High School in 1981. And then I graduated from the University of North Carolina at Chapel Hill in 1985 with a Bachelor of Science degree in Criminal Justice and Psychology. I also completed some graduate studies at Central Michigan University in 2009.

I have worked in the capacity of career counselor, camp counselor, case manager, correctional officer, and correctional treatment specialist throughout the course of my career. In hindsight, it has become my own opinion that these roles could best be served with one's ability to execute a hefty dose of humility, master versatility, and foster stern discipline. I have experienced multiple levels of management protocols, yet the waters are no less murky at the top. Our criminal justice system is sorely broken and has been out of control for many, many years.

Lastly, as President Barack Hussein Obama, one of the greatest men of our time, succinctly states, "change will not come if we wait for some other person or some other time. We are the ones we've been waiting for. We are the change that we seek."